MINDFUL NUMEROLOGY

YOUR GUIDE TO EMOTIONAL AWARENESS, PERSONAL FULFILLMENT AND DEEPER RELATIONSHIPS

KIMBERLY EATON

CONTENTS

For Mom,
My North Star

INTRODUCTION

I got married...
in my 4 Personal Year = *Building a Solid Foundation.*

I became a mother...
in my 5 Personal Year = *Transformation and New Direction.*

I got divorced...
in my 7 Personal Year = *Solitude and Introspection.*

I moved to a new city with a new job...
in my 1 Personal Year = *New Beginnings and Opportunity.*

I wrote this book...
in my 3 Personal Year = *Self-Expression and Creativity.*

When I looked back at every decade of my life, I was astonished at how my major life events were already laid out in my numerology chart, year by year, theme by theme.

When I calculated the numerology numbers for my personality, my private self, my strengths and weaknesses... Again I was astounded at the seamless way my life path dovetailed with the descriptions of my numbers.

But this is not your ordinary numerology book.

My background is in psychology. My Master's degree is in Marriage & Family Therapy. I have had a lot of psychotherapy and experience in this field. But I also love metaphysics and have studied it all my life: numerology, astrology, tarot, the afterlife, past lives, near-death experiences... I've always been peeking through the veil between worlds.

Numerology is a window into your soul's plan for you. It will give you a deeper understanding of yourself and others. It will guide you toward your highest purpose, and it is a tool for self-empowerment.

It is a science, based on physics.

But it is also a spiritual science.

I'm going to take you on a ride that you are not expecting. It's the road to your renewal.

Faith is an island in the setting sun

But proof, yes...

Proof is the bottom line for everyone.

— PAUL SIMON, *PROOF*

Keep your mind open, and by the end of this book, you'll have your proof.

1

NUMEROLOGY: THE MYSTERY AND HISTORY

The day science begins to study non-physical phenomena, it will make more progress in one decade than in all the previous centuries of its existence.

— NIKOLA TESLA, INVENTOR AND
ENGINEER

The universe has big plans for you, and it's time to understand them.

You are an eternal soul having a human experience.

The meaning of life? To gain self-awareness, share your gifts, and embody love in all its forms.

You are about to embark on a journey that blends psychology with spirituality. The plans made for your personal growth for this lifetime will be revealed so that you can do the work you came to do and live your life to the fullest.

Your life is filled with potential that you prepared for long before birth. You have the choice and the freedom to do whatever you choose with your life. Will you fulfill your potential and follow the outline for growth that you intended to, or will you exist as a smaller version of your best self?

Numerology is a tool for a deeper understanding of yourself, your relationships, and your purpose in life. It is the philosophical and metaphysical study of the vibrational meaning of numbers. The Natural Law of Vibration is the accepted scientific fact that all matter in the universe carries a unique vibration and sacred meaning.

An ancient spiritual science, numerology is imbued with inherent wisdom that is highly accurate for understanding your inner nature, talents, goals, and opportunities. You will gain insight about your strengths and weaknesses, seeing aspects of your personality that unexpectedly influence you.

You do not need to be good at math to calculate the meanings of your personal numbers. It's easy, and everything you need is here in this book.

When you understand yourself better, you can better understand others too, and recognize which opportunities are worth pursuing.

Numerology explains the cyclical patterns of our lives and the personal qualities of each individual. Numbers are symbols with their own language, explaining how ideas can be connected. Each cardinal number 1–9 represents archetypes, human characteristics that we all possess in various quantities. The endless variety of number combinations becomes the basis for each individual's unique personality.

The nine archetypal numbers symbolize the nine stages of human development we all experience to complete our spiritual growth and expansion. This time-tested science of self-discovery will enhance your life in more ways than you can imagine, as it has for thousands of years.

I am giving you a brief background of numerology, but you will see for yourself that *it just works.* You will find yourself turning to it time and again, especially to work with your themes in each Personal Year going forward.

Our numerological patterns are determined by *your birth date and your given name* (exactly as it appears on your birth certificate). Each letter of your name has a corresponding number that carries a vibration with specific characteristics absorbed over many centuries. Your birth name and date are assigned numerical values and combined to make single-digit numbers that explain your unique traits, talents, and life lessons.

This book is your guide to a practical system that will reshape your worldview. You're going to learn about numerology, of course – but also about relationships, personal growth, self-awareness, karma, past lives, and love.

I shall not commit the fashionable stupidity of regarding everything I cannot explain as a fraud.

— CARL JUNG

The history of numerology is ancient, dating back thousands of years to Mesopotamia, Egypt, and Hebrew mysticism. Though it has its roots in Kabbala, it was the sixth-century Greek mathematician and philosopher Pythagoras, the father of geometry for his Pythagorean theorem, who is considered the founder of modern numerology. His research into the relationship between music and numbers taught him that the universe has its vibrational basis in numbers, and *specifically the numbers 1-9.*

Pythagoras believed that all matter in the universe is one connected substance; all is energy moving at different rates of vibration. He discovered that *everything*—from planets to music to human beings—resonates to its unique frequency. He knew then what quantum physics now accepts—the fundamental reality that all phenomena are interdependent in the universe.

Everything in the universe is pure vibratory energy that is constantly moving. Solid matter is just energy in a specific state of vibration. Orderliness has always existed, which the rational mind may still dismiss as random, but that is usually discovered to be humanity's ignorance.

We are slowed down sound and light waves, a walking bundle of frequencies tuned into the cosmos. We are souls dressed up in sacred biochemical garments and our bodies are the instruments through which our souls play their music.

— ALBERT EINSTEIN

All natural and spiritual sciences are based on the understanding of order in the universe. This underlying unity is the basis of numerology, which can manifest for you in powerful ways. Our names and birthdates connect to our inner being in ways the intuitive mind already comprehends. We understand our lives more deeply when we interpret these numerical relationships.

All are vibrationally connected—music, harmony, and language. The act of naming something is not arbitrary. From our innate understanding of vibration, we give names to things because we associate certain qualities with the sounds of the words. We name something based on an unconscious sense of its true nature. Language represents the nature of humanity. Sound and vibrational frequency are rooted in a harmonious universal order.

In numerology, your name and birthdate reflect your actual inner being, a vibrational melody that profoundly represents who you are.

We resonate with the vibrational patterns of the numbers 1–9 through 9-year cycles, which bring specific themes and opportunities for growth. By understanding the cycles, we can learn to express our human and divine potential more effectively.

You came to this planet with a higher purpose, and numerology can offer pathways to experiencing your goal. Awareness of our particular rhythms can enable us to flow with life, work more harmoniously with others, and become the master of our fate.

All great truths begin as blasphemies.

— GEORGE BERNARD SHAW

2

THE NATURAL LAWS OF THE UNIVERSE

You and everyone else in the universe are playing the part that you have assigned to them. You can script any life you desire, and the universe will deliver to you the people, places, and events just as you decide them to be. For you are the creator of your own experience. You have only to decide it and allow it to be.

— ESTHER HICKS

There are several natural, immutable laws of the universe, which all apply to numerology.

We have already discussed the **Law of Vibration**, that everything in the universe has a unique vibrational frequency and that all things are vibrationally interconnected.

The **Law of Balance** is the law of cause and effect. It is also the law of karma. For every action, there is an equal and opposite reaction. The energy created by an act must be returned or *balanced*. I will elaborate on this in the Karmic Debt Chapter.

And, of course, there is the **Law of Gravity**, Newton's Law of Gravitation: Any particle of matter in the universe attracts any other with a force varying directly as the product of the masses and inversely as the square of the distance between them. In other words, *what goes up must come down*.

The Law of Attraction

This brings us to the most powerful law in the universe, the natural law that affects all things at all times, the **Law of Attraction:** *that which is like unto itself is drawn.* Nothing exists that is unaffected by this law, including numerology.

In Esther Hicks' book *The Law of Attraction: The Basics of the Teachings of Abraham*, there is an exact correlation between what you are thinking and experiencing. Nothing merely appears in your experience. **You vibrationally attract all of it. There are no exceptions.** Your thoughts are vibrations. The Law of Attraction responds to your thoughts and amplifies them. Whatever you focus on increases.

This is an attraction-based universe. Vibrational frequencies that match will attract each other and grow. When you set your radio dial to a specific radio station, you will receive the broadcast transmitted only from that radio station. The signals from the radio station and the receiver must match.

Whatever you give attention to is included in your vibration, and if you hold your attention to it long enough, it will manifest in your experience. The Law of Attraction responds to the thoughts you are offering. This is not philosophy. It's physics.

You might notice that those who speak mostly about illness have illness. Those who speak mostly about prosperity are prosperous. Whether you are thinking about something in your past, present, or future, you activate a vibration, and the Law of Attraction is responding to it now.

The vibrational signal you are transmitting is called your **Point of Attraction.** Your energetic thoughts are attracting other, similar active thoughts. The more you think a thought, the more habitual it becomes, and the neural patterns created in your brain are strengthened. The more you focus on positive outcomes, the more Law of Attraction will deliver you just what you ordered.

Therefore, you are the creator of your own reality.

When unwanted things occur in your experience, you may proclaim that you did *not* create such a thing and that you would never have done this undesirable thing to yourself. But though you did not *consciously* cause it, the simple fact is that only you could have caused it because *no one has the power to attract what comes to you but you.*

By focusing on the essence of something you did not want, something negative, you have created it by default. You invite it into your experience by paying attention to it, whether it is wanted or unwanted. The thoughts you think grow larger and more powerful. The larger it grows, the more power it draws unto it, and the more certain it is that you will receive the experience.

There is no exclusion in our attraction-based universe. Whether you think about what you want or what you don't want, your attention to it includes it in your vibration. Therefore, there is no such thing as "No." Your attention to anything will draw it to you.

Fortunately, things do not instantly manifest in our time-space reality, so there is a wonderful buffer between the onset of your thoughts and when they manifest. This allows you to redirect your focus back onto what you DO want to manifest, and you can tell by how you feel whether it is something you want to call into your experience.

To help you guide your point of attraction in your desired direction, the universe and divine Source Energy have given you a beautiful built-in **Emotional Guidance System.** Your soul, your wise inner being, knows your life plan and goals for this incarnation. So, if you choose thoughts that are not in harmony with your best interests, you will feel the discord within you.

Your emotions are the physical indicator of your relationship with your soul. Through your ever-present emotions, you will always know whether your thoughts are straying from your broader intentions or flowing with them. When you think about something you want, you will feel positive emotions. You will feel negative emotions when you think about what you do not want.

Because frantically trying to cancel or monitor your thoughts is impossible, you can *pay attention to how you feel.* Then, you can redirect your thoughts to something that feels better and serves you better.

You are an electronic being, far more than flesh, blood and bone. You manage your current by molding your emotions. Decide how you want to feel and create that intention. The better you feel, the better your point of attraction is, and the better things will turn out for you.

Since everything is energy, when you tune yourself and your vibration to the frequency of what you want, your reality will match. Understanding the powerful Law of Attraction is essential, especially as you learn numerology, to know how to direct your energies toward your life goals.

You can now see how vital positive thinking can be for things to go well. You must practice seeing things as you want them to be rather than continuing to observe them as they are in order to attract what you want into your experience.

Since you are flowing energy all the time, focus it out there in advance and create what happens. Otherwise, your energy is only reacting to what is happening. There is so much power in the focusing of the mind.

The highest form of ignorance is when you reject something you don't know anything about.

— DR. WAYNE DYER

3

THE SOUL'S JOURNEY

Sometimes I have believed as many as six impossible things before breakfast.

— LEWIS CARROLL, *ALICE'S ADVENTURES IN WONDERLAND*

You don't need mathematical expertise to learn the defining spiritual qualities of the numbers 1–9 and the formulas that reveal them. Once you know the basic information, you can quickly see what your soul intended to master in this lifetime—what you signed up for in this particular time and place.

It is a scientific fact that energy cannot be created or destroyed. Because energy cannot die, it can only change forms; all of life is a continuously unfolding vibrational flow. Understand that this is not your first rodeo on planet Earth. There is worldwide, ancient, and current documented evidence of reincarnation. Each life offers new lessons that the soul chooses to experience for continuous, glorious expansion.

Most people now believe in the afterlife, though many who do not know the evidential scientific research about it still have a mindset similar to "The world is flat." However, if this book is in your hands, you are likely not one of them.

Here are some opinions on the afterlife from sources you might not expect:

I am confident that there truly is such a thing as living again, that the living spring from the dead, and that the souls of the dead are in existence.

— SOCRATES

I adopted the theory of reincarnation when I was 26. Genius is experience. Some seem to think that it is a gift or talent, but it is the fruit of long experience in many lives.

— HENRY FORD

It's so silly. All you do is get the heck out of your body when you die.
My gosh, everybody's done it thousands of times. Just because they
don't remember doesn't mean they haven't done it.

— J.D. SALINGER

Live so that thou mayest desire to live again – that is thy duty – for,
in any case, thou wilt live again!

— FRIEDRICH NIETZSCHE

The number of doctors, scientists, and researchers who have found evidence for life after death and near-death experience survivors is comprehensive. A list of recommended readings by some of the breakthrough pioneers in the field is at the end of this chapter. Likewise, past-life regression therapy for present-day phobias is highly successful and on the cutting edge of modern psychotherapy.

The findings of all the decades-long scientific studies and the work of renowned and tested psychic mediums have all reached the same conclusions and reveal the same steps for the journey of souls.

According to Dr. Michael Newton's groundbreaking book, *Journey of Souls: Case Studies of Life Between Lives*, we reincarnate with other soul family members and friends in various formations to grow, learn, and support each other's development. The soul, along with spirit guide advisors and teachers, examines the lessons that must be addressed based on what has been learned in previous incarnations. The soul chooses a soul path, knowing that lessons will be presented in many ways throughout life.

With each life, you are seeking opportunities to overcome negative patterns, balance energies, and push beyond self-imposed limitations that held you back in previous lives. Your life plan provides continuous, lifelong opportunities to deliver these necessary growth experiences. Our divine plan includes joyous opportunities for expansion with other members of our soul family.

All the world's a stage,

And all the men and women merely players;

They have their exits and their entrances;

And one man in his time plays many parts,

His acts being seven ages.

— WILLIAM SHAKESPEARE, *AS YOU LIKE IT*

You can view it this way. Every life is like an elaborate Shakespeare play, as we take on different roles, enacting all the love, agony, and drama on this life's stage. The soul longs to experience life in ALL forms—the good, the bad, and the ugly. Our natural home (the afterlife realm) vibrates at an extremely high rate of unconditional love.

But we come to earth for the experience of **duality** it provides: light/dark, up/down, joy/sadness. There cannot be one without the other. You have no idea how much your soul wanted to come here for this physical experience—to feel the five senses, to touch your lover's skin, to see the sunsets, to hug the dogs, to soar with music, to taste the chocolate, and to inhale the scent of wildflowers.

We take on different roles for each other in each life to provide the most growth possible for the soul. These are called soul contracts, or soul agreements, the pre-arranged understanding we have with other soul group members to play a role that will facilitate the most growth. It is a divine merging of the soul's intended plan with the soul's inherent free will.

For example, let's say your soul has dealt with themes of power-lessness and unworthiness over many lifetimes. In this lifetime, your soul wanted to work on this and learn to feel worthy and empowered. To do that, you must first encounter *situations and people that bring out* the innate sense of unworthiness you harbor within you. Once these feelings have risen to the surface of your awareness, you can react differently and make more empowering, self-respecting choices.

Your life plan will continually provide you with opportunities to work on the specific issues you hope to gain mastery over in this lifetime. Your soul mates graciously volunteered to play any role that would help you in this cause—friend, lover, villain —no matter the part, they volunteer to do it out of deep love for your soul. Yes, even the villains in your story are soul agreements for your growth. You do the same for them in their personal stories. The orchestration of love and life plan for all of us is intricately and divinely designed.

Everything we feel and do as humans is necessary to create the rich, whole experience of life that the soul came here for. According to Robert Schwartz's *Your Soul's Plan: Discovering the Real Meaning of the Life You Planned Before You Were Born*, in the pre-life planning phase, the soul did not fear the challenges to come—indeed, the soul, in concert with spiritual guides, created the roadmap for this particular life journey. Everything is chosen to maximize specific lessons, talents, and growth that the soul can only get from the physical experience.

Some of your life script was planned, and certain relationships and situations are guaranteed on the journey you chose, but each soul **always has free will** in how they choose to participate in the play. You follow a general life map that you designed. As you reach the inevitable destiny points necessary for this plan, there are always various branches on the tree that the soul can choose in response to the event.

Though several life choices are available for a specific event, they are still *tailored to show you the lesson your soul hoped to learn from the event*. It is a beautiful synchronicity of universal intentions and your own free will once you are incarnate.

We will use the term Source, or Source Energy, to describe the divine universal source of love. God, Creator, the Universe, the Source …. we are all connected to this powerful source of love.

When souls return "home" to the afterlife, Earth's amnesia fades with all the pain and difficulty. The amnesia is necessary, or we will not entirely focus on the plans we made for the life we are enacting. Once home again, we recall how powerful and beautiful each soul truly is. We remember that there is no separation between us and the divine Source—all is one and vibrationally connected.

Then, the merry band of souls in our family group can reunite, laugh, and discuss how well we enacted that particular play and, most importantly, what each soul learned in this chosen life.

There is a scene in the movie *Tootsie* that humorously demonstrates a soul agreement. Dustin Hoffman is irritating Teri Garr during their rehearsal for an acting audition. He insists that she play her role more assertively, but she continues to read her lines meekly. He pokes and prods her until she explodes with anger at him—then delivers her lines perfectly.

TERI

That was fantastic! I felt so empowered!
Did you feel how much I hated you?!
But how will I recreate this anger tomorrow for the audition?

DUSTIN

I'll pick you up at 9:00 and enrage you.

That's what souls do for each other. There's no part too small for another soul to play for you, and vice versa. Every relationship gives you opportunities to grow. And there is always soul growth. Always.

Nothing is random. Indeed, our soul chose the time and place of our birthdate and the numbers inherent in our birth name. The numbers and planetary positions in our numerology and astrology charts are selected to maximize the soul's learning opportunities in every incarnation. You bring specific talents and knowledge gained from previous lives as a base for each new life. You also bring with you all your struggles, your traumas, and your unresolved issues.

We all come from pure love and return to pure love. Our journey on earth is a joint agreement to temporarily forget our eternal nature and focus on the lessons planned for our current life. We are here to love, play, grow, and feel *every human feeling possible*. Of course, this must include all of humanity's darkness, pain, and unfairness.

We can't learn without pain.

— ARISTOTLE

From the soul's spiritual perspective, there is no danger in these earthly experiences because we all return to the one Source after every life. The Earth plane is an illusion, a dream state from which we awake once we return home.

Once we arrive into the human perspective, the pain and difficulty inherent to the Earth plane can feel impossible to accept. However, from the perspective of your Source, humankind is progressing in ways we cannot comprehend from "down here in the trenches."

The energy of your Source, the Creator, is one of endless appreciation and bottomless love for you and your willingness to come to play on this planet and expand universal awareness. And everyone who has drifted in and out of your life was purposely chosen. Give thanks to all of these people, and seriously consider what they contributed to your experience. You are a perfect part of a vast tapestry of soul energy, with events orchestrated for your highest growth in impossibly intricate ways, weaving in and around your free will choices.

From the soul's perspective, Earth could be considered the "wild, wild west of planets." Life here is intense, so growth and expansion opportunities are very high. We come here to experience ALL the aspects of being human. Above all, the soul seeks to grow and expand to become closer to Source Energy.

Only the bravest souls seek to incarnate here, so count yourself among those courageous souls.

As one human soul evolves, progression is made in all of humankind's grand scheme. The light at the end of the tunnel is not an illusion. The tunnel is.

There is a reason for everything, no matter how it appears from the human perspective. Karmic intentions are finding their balance. There are lessons we intend to grow from that could only occur through specific situations. All is forgiven, and all is understood from the afterlife. We are never alone; we are always guided, and we need only quiet our minds and go within to intuitively feel the guidance, which can come in many forms.

Numerology is one such guide, a blueprint for your journey. Seeing the spiritual power of numbers can help you better understand all the people who have chosen to be cast members playing their roles in your life's play. You may not know what karmic role an individual plays in your life or which agreement to assist each other is underway. But as you learn your soul's goals for this life through your numerology, you can get a pretty good idea of what someone is here to teach you and why.

Knowing how well each person is aligned with their own highest spiritual purpose provides valuable insight into the quality (and challenges) of every relationship. You will see yourself and the behavior of others in a whole new light. You become the conscious creator of your life path.

The truth is the one thing that nobody will believe.

— GEORGE BERNARD SHAW

Here is a brief list of highly recommended books by just a few of the many pioneers in the field of afterlife research if you wish to begin a deep dive into this fascinating area:

Life After Life, Dr. Raymond Moody

Many Lives, Many Masters, Dr. Brian Weiss

Children Who Remember Previous Lives, Dr. Ian Stevenson

On Life After Death, Dr. Elizabeth Kübler-Ross

The Afterlife Experiments, Dr. Gary Schwartz

Science Discovers the Afterlife, Dr. R. Craig Hogan

Your Soul's Plan, Robert Schwartz

Journey of Souls, Dr. Michael Newton

If you wish to dive deeper into your own past lives, soul plans, and pre-life planning, I have personally worked with all of these gifted past-life regression therapists and intuitive counselors prominently featured in Dr. Michael Newton's bestselling books *Journey of Souls* and *Wisdom of Souls*, and Robert Schwartz's bestsellers *Your Soul's Plan*, *Your Soul's Gift*, and *Your Soul's Love*. I highly recommend the books and these talented, intuitive professionals:

Corbie Mitleid, corbiemitleid.com, Professional Psychic Medium, Past Life Specialist, Soul Plan Readings, Ordained Minister, Certified Tarot Master, Numerologist.

Staci Wells, staciwells.com, Psychic Medium, Medical Intuitive, Astrologer, Spiritual Counselor, Past Life Specialist, Pre-Life Planning Readings.

Scott de Tamble, lightbetweenlives.com, Certified Past Life Regression Therapist.

Pat Dumas, fireflyhollowwellness.com, Professional Astrologer, Tarot Master, Spiritual Intuitive.

At each shift of the paradigm, the impossible presents its impeccable credentials...and the unthinkable becomes the norm.

— RABBI MICHAEL BERG, *BECOMING LIKE GOD*

Numerology Legend

1
- Independent
- Original
- Driven
- Ambitious
- Leader
- Visionary
- Individualistic
- Determined
- Ruthless

2
- Intuitive
- Diplomatic
- Sensitive
- Supportive
- Peacemaker
- Spontaneous
- Warm
- Insightful
- Unrealistic

3
- Creative
- Communicator
- Energetic
- Inventive
- Bouncy
- Artistic
- Broadminded
- Imaginative
- Scattered

4
- Dependable
- Detail-oriented
- Predictable
- Practical
- Manager
- Problem solver
- Trustworthy
- Worrisome
- Stubborn

5
- Dynamic
- Quick-witted
- Restless
- Creative
- Adaptive
- Daring
- Persuasive
- Charming
- Procrastinator

6
- Responsible
- Caring
- Self-sacrificing
- Protective
- Helpful
- Compassionate
- Obliging
- Artistic
- Meddlesome

7
- Perfectionist
- Pious
- Careful
- Tolerant
- Thorough
- Introvert
- Spiritual
- Studious
- Obsessive

8
- Authoritative
- Entrepreneurial
- Realistic
- Planner
- Dominating
- Striving
- Forceful
- Farsighted
- Greedy

9
- Idealistic
- Political
- Aloof
- Confident
- Sophisticated
- Romantic
- Open-minded
- Generous
- Arrogant

11
- Master Dreamer
- Spiritual Illuminator
- Intuitive Teacher
- Psychic Energy
- Nervous Tension
- Idealist
- Healer
- Peacemaker

22
- Master Builder and Teacher
- Powerful Visionary
- Leader and Organizer
- High Ideals
- Large Endeavors
- Nervous Tension
- Building Utopia
- Bridging Spiritual and Material Worlds

4

THE UNIVERSAL MEANINGS OF NUMBERS

We do not grow absolutely, chronologically. We grow sometimes in one dimension, and not in another, unevenly. We grow partially. We are relative. We are mature in one realm and childish in another. The past, present, and future mingle, pulling us backward, forward, or fixing us in the present. We are made of layers, cells, constellations.

— ANAIS NIN

Similar to other practiced methods of divination, numerology can expand your perspective on the life you chose for this incarnation. It can be a valuable tool to help you understand yourself and others and empower you to follow your true purpose. Then, you can consciously work with the universe's flow to bring your best and highest self to life's table.

The numbers 1–9 represent specific character and personality archetypes. The numbers reveal your potential strengths and weaknesses, cycles, and opportunities. You will gain insight into your true nature and the reasons behind your choices. You always have free will and can choose to act from your highest potential.

We will be covering the **five core numbers** used to create your life chart through the numbers of your birth date and your birth name:

- Life Path number
- Expression/Destiny number
- Heart's Desire/Soul Urge number
- Personality number
- Birthday Gift number

Later, we will explore other numbers that can profoundly affect you: Karmic Debt numbers, Maturity numbers, and Relationship Compatibility numbers.

We will then explain your Personal Year numbers. Like the 1–9 numbers, everyone follows a 9-year complete cycle, which then repeats with the next 9-year cycle. Each year has its own energetic theme, so aligning with the energies of each year will help you maximize your opportunities and connect with the deeper meanings.

Following are the brief **universal meanings of the numbers.** As you find them in various positions in your life chart, you will see they have more specific definitions depending on their placement.

Each number has both positive and negative characteristics. Your work is to learn these tendencies and try to align them with the optimal expression of each number.

1: The Innovator

Independence, beginnings, courage, achievement... the 1 is the rugged individualist, paving the way for the rest of us. Highly motivated and ambitious, the 1 will take risks and try new things. A born rebel, the 1 is competitive and innovative.

Where balance is needed: Navigating independence vs. dependence, being self-centered, requiring more confidence, and learning to work effectively with others.

2: The Peacemaker

Loving, sensitive, intuitive, patient... the 2 is the gentle mediator, the diplomat, who seeks cooperation and guides others back to harmony. Tactful, supportive, and a good listener, the 2 can sense the energies of others and uses empathy to create balance.

Where balance is needed: Establishing healthy emotional boundaries, being decisive, feeling victimized, and learning not to be a doormat.

3: The Artist

Creative, joyful, self-expressive, uplifting... the 3 is the playful communicator, speaking their truth to inspire others. The 3 is the optimist, with dreams and artistic ideas to share. Personal connection and communication are essential to the fun-loving 3.

Where balance is needed: A tendency toward escapism, requiring discipline, overcoming self-doubt, and emotional highs and lows.

4: The Builder

Practical, stable, hard-working, patient... the 4 is grounded in reality, efficient and dependable. The 4 seeks security and is committed to building solid foundations. Disciplined and organized, the 4 is detail-oriented and likes to work step by step.

Where balance is needed: Being bossy and inflexible, lacking tolerance and acceptance, being too frugal, and learning to lighten up.

5: The Adventurer

Free spirit, risk-taker, energetic, explorer... the 5 needs exciting experiences and thrives on change. The 5 is social, charismatic, and loves new people and new environments. Daring, flexible, and curious, the 5 is enthusiastic and easy-going.

Where balance is needed: Difficulty committing to anything, learning to follow through with projects, being irresponsible and overindulgent.

6: The Caretaker

Harmonious, healing, compassionate, empathetic... the 6 is idealistic, highly nurturing, and a devoted partner. Focused on family harmony, they are fiercely protective and giving to others. The 6 is romantic, reliable, and good at making others feel comfortable.

Where balance is needed: Managing high expectations, being overbearing, seeking control, and being meddlesome.

7: The Seeker

Intellectual, spiritual, wise, analytical... the 7 seeks knowledge in all its forms, committed to inner development and self-exploration. Intuitive, private, and solitary, the 7 aims to illuminate hidden truths. The 7 is curious, seeking deep understanding, not surface frivolities.

Where balance is needed: A tendency to be aloof, cynical, emotionally disconnected, and lacking in self-confidence.

8: The Achiever

Focused, assertive, ambitious, manifesting... the 8 is the great achiever, the goal-oriented leader who finds success through determination. The 8 is associated with material wealth and prosperity. Issues with money, control, and ethics follow the 8 as they need to influence others positively.

Where balance is needed: Greed and overfocus on money, feeling victimized and disempowered, being selfish, and learning to focus on generosity and spiritual wealth.

9: The Healer

Humanitarian, visionary, generous, completion... the 9 is idealistic, empathetic, and focused on the greater good. A champion of the underdog, the 9 is tolerant, open-minded, and self-sacrificing. As 9 represents the completion of one cycle, there is a focus on forgiveness, letting go, and bringing in a new process through transformation.

Where balance is needed: You can be self-righteous, prone to wallow in misery from self-sacrifice, may have trouble letting go of the past, and can be too proud to accept help and support.

Master Numbers

If you reach an 11 or 22 in your core chart calculations, leave them in their double-digit form—do not reduce them to 2 or 4. We list these numbers as 11/2 and 22/4. Add your birthdate numbers in both ways to see what digits come up.

These are power numbers, which amplify the critical themes of their single-digit number. These numbers have a divine purpose. You are called to be more and do more. You can view the master numbers as their single-digit number ... but on steroids!

Master numbers are standard, but their intensity is for a higher spiritual purpose. You are here to bring a spiritual message to the world or to build systems to benefit humanity. This is not easy—it means you are here to step up and take the lead to master the theme. You will be challenged but given specific strengths to bring your gifts to the world. This work will unfold slowly and last throughout your life.

11/2: Master Dreamer/Spiritual Illuminator

Inspirational, intuitive, leadership, healing... As an 11/2, you are asked to embody the 1 energy (independence, administration) and the 2 energy (patience, harmony). This number is about spiritual enlightenment, and you are here to share your gifts in a way that will bring your message to the world. The master numbers push you to take on a leadership role, though the challenges required will make you anxious and uncomfortable. You will be called to use your intuition and healing abilities to benefit humanity.

22/4: Master Builder/Teacher

Creator, teacher, emotional, harmony... As a 22/4, you are asked to embody the 2 energy (patience, connection) and the 4 energy (focus, builder). A very compelling number in numerology. You need to create and build systems for the benefit of humanity. This spiritual path will push you to use your hardworking 4 qualities and sensitive, emotional 2 qualities for a higher purpose. There will be obstacles to overcome, but you have a powerful force within you to make an inspired contribution to the world.

The whole point of being alive is to evolve into the complete person you were intended to be.

— OPRAH WINFREY

5

PLAYING WITH NUMBERS

You're only given a little spark of madness. You mustn't lose it.

— ROBIN WILLIAMS

Before diving into your chart's core numbers, get your feet wet by evaluating your home address and telephone numbers. This is an easy and fun one, as you'll see below. Understanding these vibrations can give you information that you might find helpful.

Since these are not your core numerology numbers, their influence is light, but the answers might resonate with you.

Your Home Address Number

The number of your home address will explain the general mood of your home and what activities and experiences you are likely to encounter during your time at that address. Of course, there are no "bad" numbers—just the light and dark sides of each number to consider. This is an entertaining concept and not one to be taken too seriously.

Do **not** refuse to move into a home you love if the address number is not a "personal favorite" of yours. Let's be clear: there is **nothing** wrong with any particular number! The address number is just something fun to note and see if you feel the vibration of that specific number during your stay at that address.

The house number is the important piece, not the street name. Everyone on the street shares the street name, so it is not particularly influential.

To Calculate your Home Address Number

Once you calculate the number, refer to the universal number descriptions in the last chapter to find the meaning of the number.

Add together each of the digits and reduce them to a single-digit number.

For example, the address number 11046 is added this way:

$1 + 1 + 0 + 4 + 6 = 12$

$1 + 2 = 3$

3 is the number vibration of the address number 11046.

The number 3 indicates a home filled with joy, optimism, and creativity. Emotions may swing high and low, but generally, expect your time in this home to focus on communication, self-expression, and entertainment.

Your Telephone Number

The vibration indicated by your phone number will explain the kinds of communications and contacts that flow through this number.

The area code and first three digits of your phone number are not necessary here. Like the street name of your address, many people share the area code and first three digits of your phone number, which are not unique to you.

Only the last four numbers of your phone number are yours alone, shared with no one else.

To Calculate your Telephone Number

Add the four numbers together like you did with your street address:

For example, the last four digits of the phone number are 4481:

$4481 = 4 + 4 + 8 + 1 = 17$

$1 + 7 = 8$

8 is the vibrational number for this phone number.

8 is the power number, so this number will have many business contacts, financial planning, and personal power issues discussed quite frequently.

These are quick and entertaining calculations that are not too serious but are good practice to get started.

Next, we'll dive into your core numbers!

Coincidence is God's way of remaining anonymous.

— ALBERT EINSTEIN

LIFE PATH NUMBER

Run as far as you can in the direction of your best and happiest dreams across the bridge that was built by your own desire to heal.

— CHERYL STRAYED

The Life Path number is the most significant number in your chart—the date of your birth. This is your mission in this life—what you came to learn. It shows you the road you will travel—the opportunities and patterns you will experience repeatedly. This is the theme you chose to master in this life, and though you may have some natural talents in this area, you'll also have more obstacles getting there.

This broad outline for your life was established at the moment of your birth, existing in the full potential you have chosen and prepared for. You have complete free will to live your life as you choose—to embody your potential fully or to live as a less evolved version of yourself. You can decide how much effort you want to commit to tapping into your highest potential. It is a dance between planned growth opportunities for you and your free will to decide how to use them.

Mastering your Life Path purpose is your lifelong work; it is a slow-developing theme. You'll often not embody the theme of your Life Path number whatsoever! You may feel that you are, in fact, the opposite of it. But you are right on track because each number has constructive and destructive aspects, and we struggle with the challenging sides throughout our lives.

It's often tough to see the destructive aspects we are involved with. Always remember that the opposite quality of the number often pulls us, and we may not realize that there is a more optimal choice we are being encouraged to make in a given situation.

You will succeed—it's what you came to do, so keep focusing on the optimal ideas to stay on track. Look closely, and you will see that you have constantly been prodded to step into the traits of your number. Know that you chose this number and this theme precisely because these particular issues are *not* in your comfort zone, so your soul needs to grow and evolve toward this goal. It is your ultimate destination for this lifetime.

However, your chart comprises several numbers; you must know all the core numbers to make sense. You will see the fuller picture and see how the numbers all work together for you. It will become clear that all your other numbers are connected to and shaped by your Life Path number. Use your new understanding of your core numbers to funnel toward the work of your Life Path number. It is the **main lesson** you chose to learn in this lifetime.

Remember that your Life Path requires mastery, so it is the area that you will work on over and over. Embodying your Life Path is a marathon, not a sprint. Learn the key themes and stay on course. It won't be easy, but you will be given multiple opportunities throughout your life to master it.

How to Calculate Your Life Path Number

Your Life Path number is the sum of the numbers of your birth date. You will also turn the month *name* into a number (February is the second month, so the month number is 2). You will then reduce it to a single-digit number. If there is a double-digit number in your calculation, do another step to give you the single-digit number.

For example:

February 24, 1996

Month: 2

Day: 24

Year: 1996

Subtotal: 2022

Now, add the subtotal together. Keep adding until a single digit is obtained.

$2 + 0 + 2 + 2 = 6$

This is a **6 Life Path.**

Alternatively, you can write it out this way:

February 24, 1996

$2 + 2 + 4 + 1 + 9 + 9 + 6 = 33. 3 + 3 =$ **6.**

Still a **6 Life Path.**

It is helpful to try both ways of adding your birthdate. As you see, one sum reaches six by adding 2 + 2 + 2. The second way reaches six by adding 3 + 3.

Note: *If your sum is **11 or 22**, before reducing it to a single digit, keep these numbers as 11 or 22. These are Master Numbers.*

If, no matter how you calculate it, the master number does not show up, then there is none.

See the sample chart for clarity, and use the blank chart to fill in your numerology chart.

Life Path 1

You are a pioneer, an innovator, carving out your unique path in life. You are the independent one, marching to your own drummer. You want to be in charge, and nothing can stand in your way. You want to own your own business, as you intensely dislike being in a supportive role. You have so much talent and drive that you can become overly stressed. As strong as you are, you wrestle with self-confidence and the desire to belong.

You are meant to learn independence, so naturally, you will begin by struggling through dependence, feeling held back and unable to fit in. Eventually, this leads to rebellion and the search to express yourself in your powerful way. Stand tall and be yourself!

Your goal is to trust your power, problem-solving skills, and expertise. You will be tested and fall, but keep getting back up and bring your creative ideas into reality. You will achieve much in life if you have the leadership role and the chance to do things your way. Believe in yourself, trust your instincts, and boldly go where no one has gone before!

Life Path 2

You are all about love, peace, and harmony. Extremely sensitive and attuned to everyone else's emotions, you are service-oriented and so supportive that you often feel unacknowledged. Then, you end up hurt and resentful. You are the divine feminine energy, patient, and giving, but this leads to the need for validation and approval.

Relationships of all kinds form the center of your life. You need to watch your tendency to smother your loved ones. You are the one behind the scenes, making everything work smoothly. You are naturally conflict-avoidant, but you will learn how to mediate and inspire cooperative solutions. You have great inner strength, so trust yourself and use your power toward your goals.

The 2 Life Path is here to love and support others and to learn to love and support yourself by creating healthy emotional and physical boundaries. Your challenge is to get to know your desires and values and protect your heart, even as you are called to care for others.

Life Path 3

You are here to learn to express yourself creatively, communicate clearly, and share your joy and optimism with the world. Your talent for artistic expression is immense, and you love being in the limelight. You will work on refining your communication skills throughout your life—learning what you want to say and how to say it most constructively.

The 3 Life Path is naturally joyful and playful, yet ironically, it is awash in a sea of emotions you will spend your life trying to understand and manage. You hide your light in the lower emotional depths with sarcasm and cynicism. Part of your work is to experience your feelings fully and completely. Once you feel them, you must find healthy and creative ways to express those emotions.

Learning discipline and focusing on your talents while uplifting and inspiring others are your life path themes. The world needs your happiness and humor. Shine your light on the world!

Life Path 4

You are here to learn how to create a solid foundation through careful planning, moving slowly and steadily toward your goals. Security and stability are everything to you. Your mission is to build something of lasting value in your life through diligence and structure.

The 4 Life Path tends to be intelligent and serious, constantly absorbing information. It would be best if you moved patiently and methodically toward your goals. Your challenge is to learn to use systems step by step to bring order out of chaos. This will require hard work, and settling on work that truly motivates you may take time.

The 4 often deals with painful family or relationship issues that take a lifetime to heal. You have strong ideas about right and wrong and can be rigid. You like your safe routines, and adapting to change can sometimes be challenging. Try not be so cautious that you miss meaningful opportunities. You will work toward flexibility and opening up to people.

Life Path 5

You are all about freedom—you crave change, travel, experience, new people, and new environments! You make friends quickly with your upbeat personality. You feel everything intensely, drawn to all the sensual pleasures in life. You want to feel everything life offers, always running off to the next adventure.

The 5 Life Path is here to use your fearlessness to facilitate change and progress. As the thrill seeker, you will take risks and face danger, but you are here to show others by example how to live an adventurous, fearless life. You have excellent verbal skills and the ability to motivate people. You are multi-talented and feel comfortable in front of an audience.

Your need for freedom draws you to self-employment, but settling on one area is challenging. However, many friends and colleagues will boost your success once you find your niche. Your desire for constant stimulation means that you will struggle with impulsivity, self-indulgence, and addictive tendencies. A lifelong goal of the 5 Life Path is to learn to develop self-discipline and focus to use your freedom constructively.

Life Path 6

You are all about nurturing, serving others, and creating a happy and satisfying home life. You love to create a warm, harmonious environment through your artistic creativity. You are a loving partner or parent, adored by many. You are a visionary and idealist, which can lead to high expectations of others. You have much creative talent but may be so busy sacrificing for others that you do not give your own gifts enough attention.

The 6 Life Path carries much responsibility, and helping and supporting others brings great satisfaction. You are a real comfort to others and a shoulder to cry on, but to be truly helpful, you must find a balance between responsibility and interference. You will use your lifetime learning to nurture others without judging and criticizing their choices, accepting imperfection within yourself and others.

You are learning to pick people up when they fall, offer advice and compassion, yet ultimately adopt a live and let live attitude. You can do this by nurturing yourself as much as you encourage others.

Life Path 7

You are the classic intellectual and overthinker, peering into life's darkest corners to investigate and understand how the world works. You are drawn to find the answers to the mysteries of life. The analyst, the specialist, and the introvert —you need private time to process the onslaught of thoughts in your head. You are capable of great concentration and insight.

The 7 Life Path lives in a world of grounded, rational beliefs *as well as* intuitive, even psychic abilities. These approaches can conflict, having to internalize practical data while embracing spiritual awareness. You desire companionship and closeness, yet your independence tends to shut others out.

Do not withdraw from the world into your rich inner life, or you will be lonely and resentful. Unbalanced, you can appear aloof and superficial. You are learning how to balance your need for solitude with intimacy. Then, you can share your great wit and wisdom with others. Hold fast to your unique visions while remaining open to the input of those you love. Your work is to allow emotional connection, engage with the world, and trust in the flow of life.

Life Path 8

You are a powerhouse, destined for success and achievement. You know what it takes to make a business or enterprise thrive. You are set up for excellent material prosperity if you can step up to the opportunities coming your way. You inspire others, yet they may not see the vision you see, so you must guide and direct them. Life may be hard on you, but it's your choice to be railroaded by difficulties or see them as your best teachers. You are innately powerful, and you will come to embody that.

The Life Path 8 has naturally excellent management skills, and you want to be in charge. Status, luxury, and comfort matter significantly to you. You will likely face complex authority figures who teach you what not to do—especially in ethics, where you will be tested. Financial success comes more naturally to you than any other Life Path if you are diligent and dedicated to the work required.

You are here to learn self-control and resilience and to become empowered in every area of your life. You will need to overcome the opposite negative pole of feeling like a victim of circumstance and blaming others for your misfortunes. Arrogance, corruption, and intolerance are dangers on this path of power. Once you master the material world, it is paramount that you resist greed and use your power and influence to make the world a better place.

Life Path 9

You are the quirky, compassionate champion of the disenfranchised, and the savior of the underdog. You are highly charismatic, drawing people to you like a magnet. A true humanitarian, you will use your considerable creative talents in the service of helping others. The Life Path 9 contains elements of all the other numbers, so you are here to inspire others by example.

Socially conscious, you feel called to instruct everyone else on what needs to be done to bring more equality and tolerance to the world. You give to everyone but find it hard to accept help for yourself. Money can come to you unexpectedly when you are focused on giving and sacrificing for utopian goals, expecting nothing in return for your efforts. The more you give, the more you find rewards of all kinds.

The 9 signifies endings, coming full circle, and learning to let go. Often, you hold on too tightly to the past, and a lifelong lesson for you is to practice letting go without regret or bitterness. Family dynamics and enmeshment are a theme for you, and you will find your way as you approach life honestly and objectively. As your self-awareness grows, so does your ability to bring about real change on the world stage.

Life Path 11/2

You are the master dreamer, the spiritual illuminator, using your emotional sensitivity and intuition to lead on a grand scale. Remember that you embody the qualities of the 1 (leadership, independence, confidence) and the 2 (love, harmony, diplomacy).

The 11/2 Life Path is here to help and to heal through your creativity, which is less tangible and more feeling-based. Your energy is raising the vibration of the planet. Without conscious effort, you inspire and motivate people. Your very presence is healing. You are a bridge between the conscious and unconscious realms, tuned to a higher vibration that brings ideas and insight through you. This ability can make you feel self-conscious, but you are blessed with a specific role in this life. You will grow in awareness and slowly learn to maximize these opportunities. Your success generally does not begin until you mature into your forties.

Your life work is to use your independent thought and intuition to heal others yet still stay grounded within yourself. You sense your great potential but lack the confidence to realize this dream. The strength of the double 1 with the emotion of the 2 can bring self-doubt and paralysis, but you can harness this power. This is inspired leadership. Once you realize your true gifts, the rewards will be worth all your earlier trials.

Life Path 22/4

With the 4 as your foundational number, you are stable and driven. Then the 22 has the double 2 energy—very emotional and much less ambitious. As the master builder and teacher, you integrate your high ideals with your practical, detailed work ethic. You have a tremendous gift to bestow upon the world. You must use your idealistic vision to inspire and unite people, ideas, and resources toward your goal.

It is said that the Life Path 22/4 is the most powerful number vibration. You are helping people on a large scale, so push yourself to think VERY big. You will build something practical to change our day-to-day lives, manifesting something valuable, tangible, and permanent. You have an inspired vision, yet you must enact it in practical, grounded terms on the Earth plane. You intuitively know what will work and what will not in this endeavor.

You may not feel up to this task, and your emotional 2 energy may need a supportive push to move forward. Your 4 energy may get stuck in rigid thinking. Flexibility is not your strong suit, but you must make it so and allow others to contribute. Your life goal is to focus on the big picture, keeping the faith in the fundamental importance of your dream.

We know there is intention and purpose in the universe because there is intention and purpose in us.

— GEORGE BERNARD SHAW

Pythagorean Numerology System

1	2	3	4	5	6	7	8	9
A	B	C	D	E	F	G	H	I
J	K	L	M	N	O	P	Q	R
S	T	U	V	W	X	Y	Z	

SAMPLE NUMEROLOGY CHART

BIRTHDATE: <u>2/24/1996</u>

TOTALS:

VOWELS	5 9 5 1 3 1 9	33 = 3 + 3 = 6
FULL NAME	J E N N I F E R L A U R A S M I T H	86 = 8 + 6 = 14 = 1 + 4 = 5
CONSONANTS	1 5 5 6 9 3 9 1 4 2 8	53 = 5 + 3 = 8

LIFE PATH NUMBER (sum of birth month/day/year):   6

DESTINY/EXPRESSION NUMBER (sum of full name):   5

HEART'S DESIRE NUMBER (sum of vowels):   6

PERSONALITY NUMBER (sum of consonants):   8

BIRTHDAY GIFT NUMBER (birthdate):   6

KARMIC DEBT NUMBER (13, 14, 16, 19):   5

MATURITY NUMBER (sum of Life Path + Destiny):   11/2

PERSONAL YEAR NUMBER (sum of birth month/day/current year):   6

NUMEROLOGY CHART

BIRTHDATE: _____

TOTALS:

VOWELS		
FULL NAME		
CONSONANTS		

LIFE PATH NUMBER (sum of birth month/day/year): _____

DESTINY/EXPRESSION NUMBER (sum of full name): _____

HEART'S DESIRE NUMBER (sum of vowels): _____

PERSONALITY NUMBER (sum of consonants): _____

BIRTHDAY GIFT NUMBER (birthdate): _____

KARMIC DEBT NUMBER (13, 14, 16, 19): _____

MATURITY NUMBER (sum of Life Path + Destiny): _____

PERSONAL YEAR NUMBER (sum of birth month/day/current year): _____

7

DESTINY/EXPRESSION NUMBER

There's something which impels us to show our inner souls. The more courageous we are, the more we succeed in explaining what we know.

— MAYA ANGELOU

Now that you know your Life Path number, we can build the rest of the core numbers in your numerology chart.

Your Life Path number is your birthdate.

Your Destiny/Expression number is your name.

These two numbers are the most important in understanding your personal path.

Your birth name is your true musical vibration, representing the unique entity that is you. It is a reflection of your evolution through your history of lifetimes to reach the moment of your birth. Since all things begin as vibrations, your name is the musical sound of your soul. Your name is not accidental or arbitrary.

Your parents decide on your name through an often subconscious process as to what feels or sounds right, and that is because they give words to a vibration that they recognize as you, the soul that is coming through them. It is the vibrational entity that is you in words. We can reveal the hidden information in your name through your Destiny/Expression number.

Your Destiny/Expression number, which is your full name at birth, encompasses all aspects of your personality, how you express yourself, your true potential, and *the talents you will use to enact your life purpose.*

As the Life Path describes your primary purpose—**WHAT** you are here to learn and master—your Destiny/Expression number shows you **HOW** you will achieve your life purpose.

Your Life Path number and other core numbers based on your date of birth reveal the path you will walk in this life. But the Destiny/Expression number is your name, the real you, and it shows who is walking this path and the particular ways you go about the business of your life. This is the goal and potential you are aiming to fulfill every day of your life.

Remember your Life Path number purpose as you see how to utilize your Destiny/Expression number to meet those goals. Know that evolving into your Life Path purpose is slow and steady work—lessons that last a lifetime. But you will always be doing it through your Destiny/Expression number. Learning to synchronize these two numbers will significantly assist you on your journey.

How to Calculate Your Destiny/Expression Number

Your Destiny/Expression number is calculated using the *numbers represented by each letter of your name*. This is your full name, **exactly as written on your birth certificate**. You will utilize the Pythagorean Numerology System chart for your calculations.

Write out your full name as written on your birth certificate. If you are a Junior, Second, or Third, that will not be included in the calculation.

Use the name exactly as it appears on your birth certificate, even if your name was changed later or there is a misspelling or mistake. Your original name represents the energy and goals you chose for this lifetime.

Name changes, married names, and nicknames can be calculated, but these are only considered minor energies, not your original purpose and path.

Write out your name, and find the corresponding number for each letter in the chart.

Write numbers for the **vowels above** the name and the **consonants below** the name.

Next, reduce the numbers for each word down to a one-digit number. Then, add a total number for each word together to reach one final number for all the letters of the name.

For example:

| | 5 | | 9 | 5 | | 1 | 3 | | 1 | | | | 9 | | (vowel numbers) |
| J | E | N | N | I | F | E | R | | L | A | U | R | A | | S M I T H |

J E N N I F E R   L A U R A   S M I T H

| 1 | | 5 | 5 | 6 | | 9 | | 3 | | | 9 | | | 1 | 4 | | 2 8 | (consonant numbers) |

JENNIFER

$1 + 5 + 5 + 5 + 9 + 6 + 5 + 9 = 45$

$4 + 5 = 9$

LAURA

$3 + 1 + 3 + 9 + 1 = 17$

$1 + 7 = 8$

SMITH

$1 + 4 + 9 + 2 + 8 = 24$

$2 + 4 = 6$

Total the three name numbers together:

$9 + 8 + 6 = 23$

$2 + 3 = 5$

5 is the Destiny/Expression number for Jennifer Laura Smith.

Once you have calculated all your core numbers, you will see that **your Destiny/Expression number is the sum of your Heart's Desire and Personality Numbers.**

Destiny/Expression 1

Your destiny is to express your Life Path purpose through extreme ambition, leadership, and independence. You bravely go where others fear to tread. You thrive when left to your own devices because you always have innovative ways to handle life's ups and downs. Strength and perseverance create your success because you never give up.

Focused concentration and visualization help you attain your goals. You are so attached to your goals that you often refuse to see any flaws in your plans. Pride can be your downfall. But your tireless energy and commitment to your dream will keep you on track.

You express your Life Path purpose by developing your willpower and pushing through challenges with courage and determination. Strengthen your self-confidence and work on your Life Path with creativity and personal power.

Destiny/Expression 2

Your destiny is to express your Life Path purpose by bringing love and harmony to all you do. You work at developing relationships with a focus on patience and cooperation. You thrive when you are among family and friends.

You are diplomatic and subtly persuasive, with an innate radar that helps you avoid problem areas in another's personality. This diplomatic skill makes you an excellent partner and team player. You shun the limelight and leadership roles, preferring to be the power behind the throne.

You express your Life Path purpose with kindness and sensitivity. Your feelings are hurt easily—but do not allow yourself to drown in your emotions. Use your peacemaking skills to adapt to the situation and help dissipate conflicts with empathy along your Life Path.

Destiny/Expression 3

Your destiny is to express your Life Path purpose by infusing it with joy, playfulness, and a sense of humor. It would be best if you spoke with clear communication and continuously tapping into your emotions. You are destined to uplift others with your optimism and enthusiasm.

You are so imaginative and spirited that you tend to scatter your talents. Without discipline, you avoid responsibility, so you must learn to focus. Your gifted mind can devise creative solutions to problems if you narrow your energies in one direction.

You express your Life Path purpose with great talent and creative flair. You have a lighthearted demeanor and a natural way with words, but you must learn to slow down and listen. Your emotions can run away with you, so you inspire others to do the same once you've embraced authentic emotional expression.

Destiny/Expression 4

Your destiny is to express your Life Path purpose by building a solid foundation, often represented by a family, a system, or a business. You are driven to create something that will stand the test of time. Your honest and trustworthy nature inspires others and infuses your Life Path with stability and security.

Not one to take a trip without a mapped-out plan, you are reliable, systematic, and take your responsibilities seriously. You prefer the tried-and-true methods with your work and avoid the unpredictable or unconventional approaches. You are very honest and sincere but tend to be moralistic. Keep your sense of compassion and try to lighten up a bit.

You express your Life Path by achieving results through hard work. You can push through limitations and setbacks. You can be stubborn and fear taking risks, so think outside the box. Your excellent management skills guarantee that you will achieve your goals.

Destiny/Expression 5

Your destiny is to express your Life Path purpose by creating change, embracing adventure, and living life to the fullest. You bring high energy, versatility, and fearlessness to your Life Path goals.

Your life revolves around freedom. You feel called to explore all of your talents. Change excites you, while routine makes you feel stuck and held down. Life is your playground, but overindulgence and recklessness will naturally slow you down. It would be best to accept that you have physical and social limits.

You express your Life Path through exploration, focusing on freedom, and not letting others define you. Your task is to learn responsibility and self-discipline without losing your sense of adventure. You can churn through relationships quickly and become self-absorbed. Work on creating a structure for yourself that provides you with healthy limits but doesn't dampen your free spirit. Self-mastery will give you new levels of freedom.

Destiny/Expression 6

Your destiny is to express your Life Path purpose through nurturing, service, and responsibility to your loved ones. You try to be fair and accepting of others, which brings out the people pleaser in you. You tend to be a perfectionist in trying to do everything "right."

You are often overly responsible and meddling, or irresponsible and controlling. You are good at damage control and are so used to drama that you often create problems to have something to focus your energy on. Cultivate your nurturing gifts, whether it's children, animals, flowers, or gardens.

As the actual number of balance, the 6 Life Path knows how to bring harmony to opposing energies. You are likewise gifted with integrating contradictions within yourself, finding the middle ground around your internal conflicts. Finding balance means using your natural healing skills to counsel others, without impinging on or restricting their choices. You express your Life Path by balancing your desire to care for others with the need to care for yourself.

Destiny/Expression 7

Your destiny is to express your Life Path purpose through research, analysis, and finding a practical use for ideas. Despite your focus on information and data, you also have an undeniable spiritual wisdom that you continuously try to understand. You will learn to separate illusion from reality.

You hate anything superficial, which makes you critical of people who are not as profoundly informed as you are. Socializing is stressful for you, which causes you to retreat into isolation and become cynical sometimes. Finding a path to peace and balance, including deep contemplation and meditation, would be best.

You express your Life Path through intellectual and metaphysical development. You need to learn who you are and how you process the world, and you need a lot of private time to do that. You are mysterious but destined to share your wisdom with the world.

Destiny/Expression 8

Your destiny is to express your Life Path by embodying your personal power. You are destined to learn how to create financial freedom for yourself and ultimately give to others. You will be given many opportunities to step into your leadership role, marshal your resources, and achieve great things with your natural talent for business.

An excellent judge of character, you expect much of those who work for you, and you reward those who perform well. You will have to be tenacious and courageous in seeking your fortune, and you will be met with many obstacles. These are merely opportunities to see how much power you have within you. You must have gratitude for your success and find that balance between giving and taking.

You express your Life Path by using all your abilities to manifest financial abundance, yet you must walk this path with integrity. You need to use your power and influence wisely, not overfocus on money, and slip into greed and dominance. You will need to take full responsibility for yourself to claim the abundance you are meant to create.

Destiny/Expression 9

Your destiny is to express your Life Path through selflessly helping and supporting others. You want to fight injustice and transform the world for the better. You care deeply about humanity, yet your ideals are so high that people constantly disappoint you. You are highly creative and charismatic, but you struggle with resentment and aloofness.

Willing to sacrifice for your causes, you find satisfaction in doing anything that benefits the greater good. You are enriched by associating with people from all walks of life. You long for love, validation, and fame, yet this focus on your lofty visions can keep you from expressing your feelings and connecting with people one-on-one.

You express your Life Path by actively listening rather than preaching or lecturing. You tend to get stuck in sadness from the past, so your goal is to learn to heal and transform yourself and others. Your best expression is when you allow yourself to be vulnerable, show people your authentic self, and receive as much as you give to everyone else.

Destiny/Expression 11/2

Your destiny is to express your Life Path through inspired, loving leadership. This highly charged number attracts ideas and information at high energy speeds. You use your intuitive gifts and spirituality to bring your message to the world, but you need to ground yourself with stability to achieve this lofty goal.

As the bridge between the conscious and the unconscious, you are a powerful presence to others, but you must learn to control the intense energy that runs through you. Your extreme sensitivity to the lightning bolts of psychic information can cause nervous tension and emotional ups and downs.

You express your Life Path by integrating your 11 leadership skills with your 2 talents for patience and intuition. The 11 will push you into the spotlight, yet the 2 shies away from too much attention. You have much insight and illumination to share with others. Developing good boundaries to protect your extreme sensitivity is very important.

Destiny/Expression 22/4

Your destiny is to express your Life Path by using your spiritual gifts to create something of lasting value to help humanity. You are a master teacher with a big-picture vision and the ability to develop on a grand scale. Your goals are enormous. You want to leave your mark on human history with your creations.

The 22/4 has a great capacity for accomplishment, but you will be daunted by what building this dream asks of you. It is a huge struggle to come to terms with your ideal vision, and it will not begin to materialize until you are well into adulthood. Do not be deterred by limitations and practicalities. Do not back down from the challenges.

You express your Life Path through the hardworking authority qualities of the 4 and the double 2, which are highly sensitive and relationship-oriented. You are marrying spirit with material form, infused with heart and practicality. You sense that you are being called to make a massive contribution to the world, so trust that you have all the necessary tools.

When one door closes, another door opens, but we often look so long and so regretfully upon the closed door, we do not see the ones which open for us.

— ALEXANDER GRAHAM BELL

8

HEART'S DESIRE NUMBER

*You can never have a happy ending at the end of an unhappy jour-
ney; it just doesn't work out that way. The way you're feeling along
the way, is the way you're continuing to pre-pave your journey, until
you do something about the way that you are feeling.*

— ESTHER HICKS

Your Heart's Desire number (also called your Soul
Urge number) represents your soul's most profound,
innermost desires, the underlying urge, and the true
motivation that drives you. This is your core sense of yourself,
your deepest dreams. You tend to share this inner, secret self
with people only after you have established trust with them.
When you follow your heart, you tap into these desires and
feelings. Your Heart's Desire number is the reason for many of
your choices, intentions, and motivations.

These core feelings drive you on a deep level. These traits must be honored for you to be truly happy and fulfilled. Partners with compatible Heart's Desire numbers may find it easier to connect intimately. However, how you experience your Heart's Desire number has much to do with how well you (and your partner) align with your other core numbers.

Much healing can occur through accessing your Heart's Desire number. It influences the type of environment you enjoy living in and the general surroundings you choose. This number represents the areas where your soul will experience the most growth in this lifetime.

The Letter "Y" Conundrum in Calculations

The Heart's Desire number is calculated using **only the vowels** in your name, as shown below. However, we must address the issue of the letter Y here.

Vowels are A, E, I, O, U … and sometimes Y. Some numerologists never consider Y to be a vowel, and some always use it as a vowel. It will depend on the way the Y sounds in the particular word. That sound is a specific frequency, and since numerology is based on vibrational energy, the way the Y sounds is essential.

It can be a matter of personal preference, but some guidelines can assist you here:

When the Y is the only vowel sound in the syllable, it is considered a vowel. For example, in names such as Emily, Harry, and Amy and words such as key, reality, and pony.

The Y is considered a consonant if the syllable already has a vowel. Then, you can hear the word's harder "y" sound. For example: yellow, yard, yesterday, and yams.

This can be tricky depending on the word, and online numerology calculators may have conflicting processes for this, so again, use what feels right to you for the word. If the way you calculate it resonates with you, it is most likely the correct choice here.

Of course, if there is no Y in the name you are calculating, it won't be an issue whatsoever!

How to Calculate Your Heart's Desire Number

Refer to your complete name calculations from the Destiny/Expression number.

For the Heart's Desire number, we will only total the VOWELS in your name as follows:

Add the vowels together:

	5		9	5		1	3		1			9		(vowel numbers)
J	**E**	**N**	**N**	**I**	**F**	**E**	**R**	**L**	**A**	**U**	**R**	**A**	**S M I T H**	
1		5	5	6	9	3		9			1	4	2 8	(consonant numbers)

$5 + 9 + 5 + 1 + 3 + 1 + 9 = 33$

$3 + 3 = 6$

6 is the Heart's Desire number for Jennifer Laura Smith.

Heart's Desire 1

Your deepest desire is to lead. Wherever you work and whatever you do, your dream is always to take the lead. You have the courage and confidence to be in charge. You are good at evaluating others' abilities, but you still believe you would make the best choices and decisions. You harness your willpower and initiative to take independent action in every situation.

The Heart's Desire 1 wants to march to the beat of your own drummer and be a trailblazer for others to follow. You like receiving attention, and you have your own unique persona and style. You are not bothered if people find you controversial because you want to stand out and do things your way. Once you commit your energy and focus to something, you are utterly tenacious and able to overcome any obstacles. You have a strong need to achieve and be successful at whatever you do.

You will always be tested with the opposite of your true calling. You may have trouble stepping up into your power or battling selfishness or low confidence. However, you are meant to be a groundbreaking pioneer in your chosen field. With leadership as your Heart's Desire, you will not be fulfilled unless you feel you are entirely in charge of your own decisions in your life.

Heart's Desire 2

Your genuine desire is to be involved in healthy, loving relationships. You are extremely sensitive and sentimental, and you fall in love easily. Sad songs and movies can bring you to tears. You long to be needed by those who deserve your loving support. You are a natural team player, so you must create harmony and cooperation within all your close relationships.

The Heart's Desire 2 needs peace, comfort, and security in your life, especially in your relationships. You are a gentle soul who hates conflict, so you often give in when you should be asserting yourself. Learn to be decisive and stand up for what you believe in. Tactful and diplomatic, you have more power than you realize. Quiet persuasion is the way you get things accomplished.

You have good taste, a refined sense of style, and musical talent to nurture. Your challenge is oversensitivity and self-doubt, which can lead to isolation. But you will only thrive when you contribute to the group using your peacekeeping skills. Trust your intuition to find common ground with others because you have a natural gift for bringing love and harmony to any situation.

Heart's Desire 3

Deep in your soul, you are driven to inspire and uplift others through communication. You will not be satisfied unless you can utilize your artistic creativity in a public way, taking center stage and spreading joy and optimism. You are fun-loving, playful, and very witty. You are naturally gifted in the verbal arts—speaking, writing, acting, and singing.

As skilled as you are at light-hearted self-expression, the Heart's Desire 3 has difficulty communicating your serious personal thoughts and deeper feelings. Your entertaining wit can skim along the surface of things. Without a proper creative outlet for your feelings, you succumb to compulsive talking. Work on being focused so you can channel your deep feelings through artistic expression.

Knowing your deep emotions is vital to authentic self-expression for the Heart's Desire 3. When communicating from the heart, you are healing and uplifting others. You will battle with mood swings and scattered energies. True satisfaction will only come when you allow your soul to flow through you to reach others, which requires some focus and direction with your creative talents. Your artistic self-expression has the potential to provide you with a fascinating and successful life.

Heart's Desire 4

Your core desire is to build a solid and stable foundation for yourself. With your practical, reliable nature, you inspire trustworthiness in others. You work hard to create something valuable that makes you feel safe and grounded, and you methodically go after your dreams step by step. The Heart's Desire 4 craves structure and security and dislikes change. Too much freedom feels chaotic to you.

You carefully analyze problems and resolve them with a logical, practical approach. Your need for orderly, well-defined systems can make others feel inhibited. Be careful not to take your need for order and discipline too far. You are so dependable and energetic that you can quickly become a workaholic. You want love and a family connection but may have difficulty expressing your feelings.

It would be best if you confronted your tendency toward stubbornness and fear of taking risks. You will not feel fulfilled unless you build a family or partnership through marriage or a business partner. You are a pillar of strength and must put down roots to fulfill your heart's desire.

Heart's Desire 5

Your innermost desire is to drink deeply from the cup of life, diving into every possible adventure and soaking up every last drop of juicy life experience. The need for freedom, stimulation, and liberation from restrictions guides you. Your endless curiosity pulls you from one exciting thing to the next, especially in relationships.

With your sharp mind and way with words, you're a great communicator, thriving on variety and new ideas. The Heart's Desire 5 is not threatened by change, which is lucky because change is the only constant in life. You adapt quickly when hit with the unexpected, pivoting easily to whatever new situation arises. Consequently, you get bored easily and have a hard time finishing tasks.

Your race through life can break many hearts along the way, with your dramatic entrances and inevitable exits. Freedom is genuinely essential to you. Life can feel chaotic and out of your control at times, especially around addictive tendencies. Ultimately, you must embrace change yet stay strong when the going gets tough. You learn best through experience, which will give you significant personal growth. You desire to show others how to live fearlessly, and you will not be happy unless you are free to pursue the next quest that calls to your heart.

Heart's Desire 6

The Heart's Desire 6 has an intense need for domesticity—to nurture your loved ones in a lovely, harmonious home. Since you intuitively sense what others need even before they do, you are an expert counselor and shoulder to cry on. You need to be needed (service with a smile!) and thrive when you see your efforts rewarded in the happiness of others. You dream of a harmonious home with all social interactions filled with love.

The 6 is the most loving number, and your deep desire is to love and be loved in return. People do appreciate all the love you give. You often sacrifice your needs to give to others and risk interfering in their lives or smothering them with too much attention. Especially with your children, consider allowing them more space to cultivate their strength.

You are an artistic visionary who creates beautiful surroundings and builds your home nest. You will not feel fulfilled unless you can do this for your loved ones. However, your romantic vision of life can be unrealistic, leading to judgment and resentment. Know that giving your best to others requires putting yourself first and modulating your sense of responsibility. Then your natural loving compassion will shine.

Heart's Desire 7

Your burning desire is to discover the meaning of life. You want the answers to life's biggest questions and will not be satisfied unless you seek out this knowledge, analyze it, and discover profound spiritual truths. Your soul is on a private journey, seeking your wisdom. The idea of a hermit or monk with a quiet life devoted to study and meditation may feel like a good fit for the Heart's Desire 7.

Your inner self is mysterious and reclusive, making it difficult for others to get to know you. This can lead to cynicism, superficiality, and loneliness. You distrust feelings, so you tend to keep your relationships impersonal. You prefer to be rational and discuss facts and ideas. Emotions, in general, are cloudy and messy for you, and this is your weakness. You need to be courageous, open up, and share your heart with someone. This is a significant challenge and crossroads in your growth.

This type of connection does not come naturally, but you can create a genuine relationship with someone without sacrificing your necessary private time. Ultimately, you do desire to share your newfound truths with others. Use your fantastic powers of observation to focus on what others might also need and allow some fun into your life.

Heart's Desire 8

Deep down, you need to achieve personal power and financial security because you crave the freedom and options that prosperity provides. The money is not enough; you also want influence and energy to make a positive difference. You are a visionary and dream of huge projects that bring massive rewards.

You have the drive and the focus to carry out your big plans but need help from others to handle the more minor details. You must lead by example, bringing out the best in those who work with you to use their talents toward realizing your dreams. Your determination and desire for excellence inspire everyone around you.

The Heart's Desire 8 needs to succeed in the material world to heed your soul's calling. Corruption and selfishness will beckon, so stay focused on using your abundance for the greater good. The highest use of your power is to know the right level of involvement in your projects and act with integrity. You are in a unique position to help a great many people through your efforts. When you take the lead and tap into your sense of personal empowerment while giving generously to those in need, you will fulfill your soul's desire.

Heart's Desire 9

Humanitarian service is your deepest inner calling. You must raise your consciousness and lift everyone around you to improve the world. You have high ideals and expectations of yourself with your need to relieve the suffering of others. You love to study all kinds of people, though you will learn that not everyone has the same high values.

You are a natural counselor and teacher. You want to serve others, but you also crave fame and attention from everyone. Your high expectations can, at times, come off as arrogant. This can prevent you from truly hearing and connecting with the people you are trying to help. When others don't meet your ideals, you become resentful. Forgiveness is one of your major life lessons.

Using your wisdom and deep empathy, you are here to heal others and yourself in powerful ways. This can be a rocky road as you tangle with issues from the past and must learn to let go without bitterness or resentment. Family enmeshments can pull you down. It would be best if you took the high road, as you can come off as being preachy at times. The Heart's Desire 9 must serve others and gracefully let go of what no longer serves you. Allow yourself to accept help from others and let them in. You deserve to receive as much good as you are giving.

Heart's Desire 11/2

As the spiritual messenger, your deepest desire is to use your connection to the spiritual realm to form meaningful relationships that are a source of healing for people. In this way, you need to take the lead to help others, though often you want to be taken care of yourself. You will learn to manage this heightened energy by trusting your intuition.

Even as a child, you were wise beyond your years, deeply aware of people's thoughts and feelings. You feel a powerful calling to the metaphysical world and the less traditional routes to enlightenment. You have a highly charged, electric thought process, which can cause you anxiety and nervous tension. Many Heart's Desire 11/2s were emotionally scarred in childhood, which created deep empathy for the suffering of others and a need to be of service. You have a specific gift to share with the world that will take many years to fully comprehend.

You will create deep relationships and harmonious environments with the 2 energy you carry, but the Master number 11/2 is supercharged spiritual energy. You need rest and a peaceful home environment to settle your internal intensity. It would be best to have healthy emotional boundaries to balance your need to serve with your need to honor your intuitive powers.

Heart's Desire 22/4

Your innermost need is to transform the world by building something life-changing and then teaching others how to maintain it. You will use your leadership and organizing skills to define important goals and share your knowledge of system-building. You are using the stable 4 energy with the double 2 energy—balancing your hard work with the need to create harmonious relationships.

Early in life, you became aware of an enormous potential within you—a great power you could not understand at that time, and that caused you discomfort. Once you embody your strength, your creative ideas and leadership skills greatly inspire others. You are meant to build something that has a lasting impact on the world. Your accomplishments will be significant, but you must remain humble and focus on achieving your dream.

The Master 22/4 is an intense number, and it asks you to create your stable foundations—but do it by bringing everyone else into your plan. You may put a lot of pressure on yourself to succeed. But you will only be fulfilled once you push through your limitations and use your spiritual gifts to lead others to your vision.

Love is the ability and willingness to allow those that you care for to be what they choose for themselves without any insistence that they satisfy you.

— DR. WAYNE DYER

9

PERSONALITY NUMBER

Love yourself first and everything else falls into line. You really have to love yourself to get anything done in this world.

— LUCILLE BALL

Your Personality number is the total of the consonants of your full name. It describes your outward traits, general demeanor, and the parts of yourself you feel comfortable sharing with the world. This is a narrower, more protective aspect of the real you, how other people perceive you, the face you choose to show to the outside world. Your Personality number is the external way you present yourself.

You use your Personality number as a screening device for what kinds of information and people you allow into your world. The traits of your Personality number are used to censor which energies you choose to send out but also to welcome things that resonate with the natural inner you.

This is the entrance to your true nature and people's first impression of you. You feel safe showing this side of yourself to others, and with time and trust, you may show them the inner you—your Heart's Desire and Expression.

Your Personality number also hints at your style and how you dress. Accepting and embracing this outward energy is an essential step in self-care. Embody these traits and have fun with them!

Remember that consonants represent your public persona (Personality), vowels denote your innermost feelings (Heart's Desire), and the total of all the letters of your name makes up your Destiny/Expression number—the person you aim to be.

How to Calculate Your Personality Number

Again, using the numbers found in your name, we will calculate the Personality Number by totaling ONLY the CONSONANTS:

				(vowel numbers)
5 9 5	1 3 1	9		
J E N N I F E R	L A U R A	S M I T H		
1 5 5 6 9	3 9	1 4 2 8	(consonant numbers)	

Adding the consonants:

$1 + 5 + 5 + 6 + 9 + 3 + 9 + 1 + 4 + 2 + 8 = 53$

$5 + 3 = \mathbf{8}$

8 is the Personality Number for Jennifer Laura Smith.

Personality Number 1

People see you as an independent leader of the pack. You are driven to achieve, which inspires others to follow your original ideas. Others see you as dynamic and capable, not one who can be easily pushed around. You can come off as rebellious, even domineering, and stir up drama to get attention and praise. Others take note of your courageous choices and determination to succeed.

People recognize you as a risk-taker and pioneer in whatever you do. You can come off as intimidating and aggressive, so consider softening your approach to people. You are a snappy dresser and leave a memorable impression with your unique style.

Personality Number 2

You present as a kind, friendly, and cooperative person. People are drawn to your warm, unthreatening demeanor. You are seen as an excellent companion, attentive listener, and peacemaker who avoids arguments. People notice that you can be oversensitive with your deep concern for what everyone is thinking and your desire to provide whatever they need. You are much stronger than you appear.

You are seen as a graceful, refined person of excellent taste. You long for emotional connection, so you take great care with your appearance to be attractive to others. Your clothing leans toward soft, comfortable, flowy fabrics.

Personality Number 3

You are considered a highly attractive and natural-born entertainer—friendly, witty, and intelligent. You are a joy to be around, and people gravitate naturally to you to bask in your happy spirit. Your personality sparkles when you're in the spotlight and using your expressive skills to uplift others. However, when you feel bogged down with emotion, everyone senses it.

You are romantic, affectionate, and giving, but prone to drama. Try not to scatter your attention, as your natural wit can appear superficial. Work on developing deeper relationships. You appreciate fine clothing and jewelry. You love going to events that allow you to dress up with glitz and glamour.

Personality Number 4

You give the impression that there's nothing you can't fix, figure out, or accomplish. People know you can be trusted to keep your promises and will do whatever it takes to get the job done. You are viewed as a solid family person and protector. You present as someone who values consistency, correctness, and control.

You are super organized and good at keeping lists, so others tend to rely on you to handle the nitty-gritty details, even though you may gripe about handling everything. You want to be judged by your performance and not your appearance. Your fashion sense is mainly centered on the conventional, practical, and comfortable. You could benefit from loosening up and letting your light shine.

Personality Number 5

People see you as enthusiastic, adventurous, and constantly on the move. You appear fearless and quickly adapt to change, which intrigues others and inspires them to take risks in their own lives. You are known as a charmer and a great conversationalist—you're definitely on everyone's party list. You radiate charisma and a nervous energy that keeps pulling you to the next new experience.

You are attractive with a strong, graceful body. It would be best if you learned discipline, as you are drawn to overindulgence in all the sensual pleasures of life. You are seen as lucky and successful, but all this rushing around keeps you from a deeper understanding of your life. Everyone knows that you are a free spirit and can't be contained, and your fashion style is bold, colorful, and exciting—even risqué.

Personality Number 6

Others view you as the warm and supportive parental figure everyone turns to for advice and comfort. People sense your compassion and kindness and come to you with their burdens. Highly nurturing, you love to create beauty in your surroundings. Others know that your home life is your primary focus, and you can be counted on to help anyone in need.

People notice that you are often a perfectionist, can overdo your sense of responsibility, and become controlling and overly involved. You are not always the best judge of character; you see the best in people. But your need to sacrifice so much for others sometimes puts you in the martyr role. You are more focused on your personality than your appearance, preferring casual, comfortable, and practical fashion.

Personality Number 7

People see you as profound, mysterious, and independent. You're constantly analyzing data, and studying the nuts and bolts of how things work. You're a keen observer of everything around you, though others may read that as arrogance or even superficiality. People notice your tendency to use sarcasm quite often.

Others notice your intelligence and wisdom quickly, but you are a hard person to get to know. People know you are not one for idle chit-chat unless you find the topic fascinating. You have insight and an intuitive understanding of spiritual issues. You are too focused on other things to be concerned with personal style unless you choose to make a specific impression. You always appear dignified and well-groomed.

Personality Number 8

You give the impression that you are powerful, in control, and confident. You are a natural and effective leader, which causes others to defer to you. People see that you value money and attract abundance more quickly than most. You radiate strength and competence, attracting people with the resources that help you in business.

People know you can be warm, spontaneous, and generally well-liked. Your ego can get the best of you, making you greedy and intimidating. Success is stimulating; you want others to join in your excitement. For your personal style, only the best will do. How you present yourself matters significantly, and you like to dress well in refined, high-quality clothing.

Personality Number 9

You have an elegant, noble bearing and are aware of how you appear to others. People see you as a charismatic champion of the underdog and will follow you willingly to help with whatever humanitarian cause you believe in. You are seen as kind and generous, even quirky, with an unusual flair. You care deeply about helping others, so much so that you can burn out and be drained by your overcommitment to the cause.

People see you as a giver who can be fanatical, even arrogant, about creating large-scale change. You are better at addressing grand social issues than you are at one-on-one relationships. You give the impression of being helpful, calm, and controlled, yet you are vulnerable and sensitive underneath. Your clothing style and home environment reflect your artistic talent and excellent taste.

Personality Number 11/2

Like the 2, you are seen as emotional and giving, but with an intuitive, spiritual energy that makes people feel relaxed in your presence. You want to bring others into your lovely vision for the world. People see you as an excellent therapist with your deep understanding of human nature. However, you tend to be very personally vulnerable and unable to handle criticism well.

You give the impression that you are an easy mark and find it hard to say no. Working on your self-confidence and embracing your powerful, intuitive nature is essential. You have an intense inner spiritual life, which makes you kind, compassionate, nervous, and jumpy at times. Your style of dress tends to be soft, dreamy, and ethereal.

Personality Number 22/4

As 22/4 is the most powerful number in numerology, people quickly sense that you are deeply driven to accomplish essential things that will help others. Your strength and tenacity are second to none, and others can get swept up in your vision for improvement on a large scale. Some people may take note of your stubbornness, but no one can deny the strength of your energy. Your style is less about fashion and more about what works best for the work that must be done.

It doesn't necessarily ever get easier. You just get better at managing what's hard.

— MARK MANSON

10

THE BIRTHDAY GIFT NUMBER

I think you end up doing the stuff you were supposed to do at the time you were supposed to do it.

— ROBERT DOWNEY, JR.

Your Birthday Gift number is simply the number of the **day of the month** in which you were born. The Birthday Gift number indicates a special gift or talent you brought into this life. It is a gift you are meant to use to help you learn your Life Path's lessons. This number's energies are best used when you carry them forward into your Life Path purpose.

Your Life Path number is the main goal you came to achieve, one you need to master because it is not an area in which you have strength or expertise. In this life, you aim to change that by learning the lessons of the Life Path and gaining strength and power with your new experiences.

The Birthday Gift number is a *minor* lesson you're here to study. It's a number with traits you're more comfortable and familiar with from previous lives. This number may or may not feel in sync with your other core numbers, but it is part of your identity. As with all numbers, you swing between positive and negative poles as you seek balance and alignment with the optimal qualities of the number.

How to Calculate Your Birthday Gift Number

For birthdates from the 1st to the 9th of any month, the Birthday Gift Number is the same one-digit number, 1–9.

For example, for June 3, your Birthday Gift Number is 3.

For birthdates from the 10th onward, add the two digits together to make one digit.

For example, for June 15, add 1 + 5 = 6. Your Birthday Gift Number is **6**.

See below to match your birthdate on the right with the correct gift on the left.

Gift 1 – Birthdates 1, 10, 19, 28

With the 1 Birthday Gift, you are an ambitious leader with a creative mind driven toward achievement. You are strong and not afraid to take risks. You want to go where no one has gone before! Naturally independent, you prefer to work alone, though you are good at inspiring others to follow your vision.

You have great instincts and could manage any business. The lower vibe of this number is laziness and procrastination, or forcing the issue when things don't go your way. Your ultimate gifts are your willpower, leadership, and innovative ideas.

Gift 2 – Birthdates 2, 20

The 2 Birthday Gift is diplomacy, kindness, and sensitivity. You are a natural mediator, sensing what each person thinks before they even say it. You have a knack for bringing peace and harmony to the group dynamic. You know how to get different viewpoints together to find that common ground, but you prefer to work behind the scenes.

You love to be in beautiful environments that make you feel warm and secure. You seek relationships where your thoughts and feelings are valued. You love to give and receive praise and affection, but you are highly vulnerable and easily hurt by others. Developing inner strength and loving connections is the best use of your gift.

Gift 3 – Birthdates 3, 12, 21, 30

With the 3 Birthday Gift, you are a highly gifted, creative person with artistic talents in performing, writing, art, sales, or anything in entertainment. You are energetic, upbeat, and charming—just a lot of fun to be around. Self-expression is vital to you.

The downside is the emotional rollercoaster, scattering your energies so you can't complete your projects. You tend to wallow in depression when you feel stuck and emotionally blocked. The best use of your gift is to master your communication skills and express yourself freely and creatively.

Gift 4 – Birthdates 4, 13, 31

You are the one who always takes care of business. Super-responsible, dependable, and organized, you take your work very seriously; others know they can rely on you to come through for them. You are highly disciplined and always meet your obligations with a slow and steady focus. The 4 Birthday Gift is rational and pragmatic—not a big dreamer or risk-taker.

You are very family-oriented, and commitment comes easily, yet you are not very emotional or demonstrative in your relationships. You can be stubborn and rigid, preventing you from seeing solutions or new ideas that might solve problems. Your gift is creating stability and security and becoming more flexible with your methods.

Gift 5 – Birthdates 5, 14, 23

You love adventure, variety, travel, and change. You yearn to see the world and meet new people from all walks of life. You want to have fun and are fearless in pursuing excitement and exploration. You have a quick and curious mind with excellent communication skills—you're a natural at speaking, writing, or anything involving sales. Highly adaptable, you tend to get restless and bored quickly.

The 5 Birthday needs variety and stimulation, often to excess, by overindulging your senses. You are the proverbial drama queen or king, demanding constant attention. You usually follow your desires and impulses, no matter what the consequences—even if it means self-sabotage. Your ultimate gift resides in creating the exciting freedom your soul craves while taking responsibility for yourself with some semblance of order and discipline.

Gift 6 – Birthdates 6, 15, 24

You have a loving energy, focusing on home, family, and nurturing others. You are fiercely protective of those you care for. You have talents as a healer and a great appreciation of beauty and art. You are here to learn about proper balance and how opposites can harmonize. The 6 Birthday must understand where you can best be of service and know your limits.

You tend to carry the world's weight on your shoulders and expect much from yourself and others, who often disappoint you. You can be a control freak and a perfectionist, giving too much and then resenting when they become overdependent on you. Your ultimate gift is in giving love that is balanced with healthy boundaries.

Gift 7 – Birthdates 7, 16, 25

You have a superior intellect and a significantly developed analytical mind. You are great at researching and seeking answers to life's mysteries. You would use your intellectual gifts well by deep-diving into one field and gaining expertise. Learning to blend your rational mind with your considerable intuitive skills would be best. You seek spiritual awareness and higher meaning. Meditation or any spiritual practice will serve you well.

The 7 Birthday has deep feelings but is not adept at sharing and communicating your feelings efficiently. You like to be alone but should guard against becoming cynical, withdrawn, and self-centered. The best use of your gift is trusting others and finding a balance between your rational and intuitive awareness.

Gift 8 – Birthdates 8, 17, 26

You excel at business with sound judgment and natural leadership abilities. You are ambitious and will take daring, creative risks in building your fortune. You value the freedom and options money provides, so material abundance is necessary to feel truly satisfied. You crave status and respect and want to take your rightful place among other movers and shakers. You are competitive and not afraid of a challenge, so you can prove the doubters wrong. The 8 Birthday is a natural manager and authority figure.

You can be bossy, controlling, and obsessed with your work. You have no patience for people who lack your intense level of commitment. You will face many obstacles that require you to develop perseverance and tenacity. Your ultimate gift is creating financial prosperity by learning to empower yourself in all areas of your life.

Gift 9 – Birthdates 9, 18, 27

You are profoundly compassionate and charitable, and you will work tirelessly to make the world a better place. You are a gifted artist and humanitarian with a charisma that helps you connect easily with people wherever you go. The 9 Birthday has a vital societal role that will bring about much-needed change and transformation. You find deep personal reward in serving humanity, and you must find the best way for you to be of service to the world.

Social movements, politics, environmentalism—anything that stirs your idealistic soul would be a good fit for you. Sacrifice and forgiveness will be important themes, and you must guard against fanaticism and resentment. Your gift is to trust the universe's timing and use your creativity to serve others selflessly.

Gift 11/2 – Birthdates 11, 29

You are a spiritual visionary, so sensitive that you can intuit what other people need through your psychic abilities. The Master numbers are leadership roles, so the 11/2 Birthday Gift is about healing and inspiring groups of people, uplifting everyone in your presence. You have a knack for making spiritual growth feel accessible and easily understood by the masses.

You can have difficulty fending off the negative energy of your surroundings, which is why you crave peaceful areas for spiritual practices and artistic pursuits. You aim to please and crave praise and admiration. The best use of your gift is less emotional reactivity and tuning your awareness to lead others from a place of alignment.

Gift 22/4 – Birthdate 22

You have infinite potential as the visionary who creates a business or institution that significantly impacts the world. You are a great teacher and organizer, and you have absolute power within you to manifest your higher vision on the earthly plane. The Master 22/4 Birthday can see beyond the mundane details required and know how to build something valuable that will stand the test of time.

This intense energy can make you feel inadequate to the huge visions in your head, but do not give up on your dream. Stay the course, and you will overcome the inevitable obstacles. Your ultimate gift is to bring your goals to life and dedicate yourself to tangibly lifting humanity.

Thomas Edison's wife told me that as her husband was dying he whispered to his physician, "It is very beautiful over there." Edison was a scientist, with a factual cast of mind. He never reported anything as fact until he saw it work. He would never have reported, "It is very beautiful over there," unless, having seen, he knew it to be true.

— NORMAN VINCENT PEALE

11

KARMIC DEBT NUMBER

The most terrible and beautiful and interesting things happen in a
life. Whatever happens to you belongs to you. Make it yours. Feed it
to yourself even if it feels impossible to swallow. Let it nurture you,
because it will.

— CHERYL STRAYED

s numerology is based on the ancient idea that our souls incarnate on Earth many times to evolve, inevitably, we must address the issue of karma.

Let's clear up a misconception about karma.

Karma is not wrong, and it is not a punishment!

Karma simply means *intense energy*, which is neither good nor bad. It is the spiritual Law of Balance, the law of cause and effect. For every action, there is an equal and opposite reaction. The energy created by an act must be returned or *balanced*. With every decision you make, you shape your life. Since the cause and effect are one, if you participate in the cause, you will always participate in its effect. *As ye sow, so shall ye reap.*

Our souls bring the wisdom we learn from our past lives into each new incarnation to evolve spiritually and learn the lessons we planned for this life. But we also carry old burdens from our past lives—mistakes, abuses, and poor choices.

Understanding your Karmic Debt number is a gift. It is called Karmic Debt because you have a debt to pay for actions you took in a previous life. One of the great things about numerology is that it gives you the basic knowledge of where your Karmic Debt is located. This puts you at a considerable advantage. It can explain why you have particular struggles repeatedly.

Your soul chose all your core numbers for lessons you intended to learn, but the Karmic Debt number is high-intensity. Karmic Debt numbers are ubiquitous; most of us have one in our chart, myself included. Again, it is not a punishment. It's a significant growth opportunity for you.

You constantly create karma with your thoughts, words, and actions, consciously or unconsciously. You must be aware of your choices, make decisions from your heart, and consider whether your preferences will serve you and others. Good karma will follow you through your incarnations just as "bad" karma will.

Your choices and decisions are your instructions to the universe, which will treat you how you ask to be treated. When you inflict suffering, you will also experience suffering. Likewise, when you create joy, you will also experience joy. *You always experience the effects of your choices.* In that way, karma is the gift of awareness.

You cannot create karma for someone else; you can only make your own. You may see someone suffering and assume that it's his karma and he must deserve it, so you ignore his suffering. Indeed, you do not know what his karmic circumstances are or what healing may be occurring there, and it is not your role to judge. But if you are indifferent to the suffering of others, by the law of balance, you are creating a world where others will ignore *your* suffering.

Behave compassionately and do what you can to help others in need, but do not judge the people on either side. You end up creating karma in which you will be judged in return. The finest karma you can make is to be compassionate with everyone you see, as you will then be treated with love and compassion in return.

The universe doesn't punish you with painful circumstances. Difficult situations occur so that you can experience the consequences of your behavior and choices. The universe is compassionate by allowing you to experience what you create. This is how you can learn to use your power more wisely. Karma is always fair, reflecting who you are right back to you. Your reflection cannot change until *you* decide to change it.

In this life, you seek to balance the scales in an area of your life that requires attention due to the law of cause and effect. Karma is all about balancing the scales. If you have a karmic number in your chart, it just means that you are working on specific intensified issues you seek to balance in this life.

The energy of karma must be balanced, but it can also be transmuted. It is not always "an eye for an eye." The balance effect may not be the same infraction as in the previous lifetime. But something of equal intensity will elicit the same emotions within you that you created for another. Your life choices and your positive intentions have a significant effect on how this plays out. Focusing on forgiveness and finding things you are grateful for are optimal ways to release karmic energy.

Rather than feeling like a victim of circumstances, you can be empowered by taking responsibility in this lifetime to come to terms with the Karmic Debt. You will have to work hard at it, but that is precisely what your soul hoped for—that you would transform yourself, do what is required, and balance the coffers.

When you view your life circumstances as the natural unfolding of karma, you will not take things so personally or blame others so quickly. You can respond in ways that create positive karma by seeing others with gratitude. When you intend to respond compassionately to your experiences, you invite karma to expand your awareness and open your heart.

You may not remember the specifics of the infraction from a previous life. Still, your Karmic Debt number will point you to the area that requires your attention, and you will likely recognize your behavior patterns immediately. This is a positive thing because now that you can identify it, you can take the reins and clear your karmic slate. Increased self-awareness is the best gift of all.

Maybe you have been subconsciously working on these issues and have made significant progress already, an accurate marker of your spiritual evolution and maturity. You will appreciate your growth when you realize you have come to terms with an aspect of yourself and your behavior that no longer gives you problems.

Karmic Debt numbers are ultimately meant to bring you closer to your higher purpose. Remember that everything happens FOR you, not TO you. Your soul planned this because you must find balance in this area. This is powerful knowledge to have. You can break the cycle and find peace. You are the creator of your reality. See the Karmic Debt as an intense opportunity, and use it for your self-empowerment.

The primary cause of unhappiness is never the situation but your thoughts about it.

— ECKHART TOLLE

How to Calculate your Karmic Debt Number

A Karmic Debt number can be found in any of your core numbers, but it has the most influence if it is in your Life Path number calculation. The result is reduced if the Karmic Debt number is found in your other core numbers (Destiny/Expression, Heart's Desire, Personality).

Karmic Debt numbers are not calculated through addition as the other numbers are.

The numbers indicating Karmic Debt are **13, 14, 16, and 19.**

When we reach those double-digit numbers, we reduce them to **4, 5, 7, or 1.**

Do you have a 4, 5, 7, or 1 in your core numbers (your Life Path, Destiny/Expression, Heart's Desire, Personality)?

Look back at the calculations you made to find your core numbers. Find the sums in your name and birthday **before** you reduce them to single digits.

For example:
June 8, 1964
June = 6
Day = 8
1964 = 1 + 9 + 6 + 4 = 20
6 + 8 + 20 = **16**
1 + 6 = 7

In this example, the double-digit number 16 was reached before being reduced to the single-digit number 7.

16 is a Karmic Debt number.

The other way to reach the number 7 is by adding 3 + 4. However, **only** if the calculation reaches the number **16,** which is reduced to 7 by adding 1 + 6, can it create the Karmic Debt number.

If you can reach the single-digit numbers 4, 5, 7, or 1 *by any other method*, it does **not** create a Karmic Debt number. Before reduction, your sums must naturally reach **13, 14, 16, or 19.**

The 4 must be reached by 13, not by 2 + 2. The 5 must be reached by 14, not by 3 + 2. The 7 must be reached by 16, not 3 + 4, and the 1 must be reached by 19, not 1 + 0.

NOTE: If your birthday is actually on the 13th, 14th, 16th or 19th of the month, these are indicators of Karmic Debt with no further calculations required.

All four Karmic Debt numbers have their basis in *acts of self-ishness.*

There are four karmic themes:

Morality

Freedom

Love

Power

When the karma of a relationship is done, only love remains. Let go. It's safe.

— ELIZABETH GILBERT, *EAT, PRAY, LOVE*

Karmic Debt Number 13/4 - Morality

The Karmic Debt number 13/4 indicates a severe abuse of *morality* in a previous life. This means that you are now paying back for the suffering you caused others by being verbally abusive, judgmental, superficial, greedy, and lazy. You did not take personal responsibility for your share of the workload.

Since the infraction in the Karmic Debt is based on the numbers 3 and 4, in your current life, hard work and diligent effort will be required while roadblocks are repeatedly placed in your path. You are also being asked to learn the art of positive expression with your words: to think before you speak, not be critical, and to use your words to uplift and support others. This time, you must shoulder most of the workload AND do it with a happy attitude!

Those with the Karmic Debt number 13/4 may feel they are working hard to accomplish every task, yet success still feels out of reach. Your efforts feel futile, and you may want to give up and fall back into negativity and laziness. But success is attainable if you buckle down and persevere. Many successful people from all walks of life have a Karmic Debt of 13/4, and focus is the key to their good fortune.

The 3 energy influence in the 13/4 here is the tendency to scatter your energies. But this Karmic Debt number requires endurance and responsibility for your thoughts, words, and actions. You must learn to concentrate and focus your energy in one direction, which requires keeping things in order. Keep your work area tidy, keep all your appointments, communicate clearly and concisely, and follow through with your commitments.

Ongoing health problems can be an issue for the 13/4 Karmic Debt number. You will need self-discipline to take good care of yourself, eat well, exercise, and meditate to find balance. Exhaustion is common here, so pace yourself because no matter what else is going on, you still need to push through and overcome these obstacles.

It feels like you are being tested, and you are. Commitment is required, and there are no two ways about it. You are asked to revise how you communicate with people, use your creativity to manifest positive results, and use all your considerable skills to bring a complex project to fruition—and do it all with a smile.

There are no shortcuts or easy ways out of the Karmic Debt number 13/4. You will learn accountability in this lifetime, AND you must bring a sense of lightness and joy to your work —to whistle while you work, as it were. That may sometimes feel impossible, but you have the gifts of the 3 and 4 to work with: positive self-expression, creativity, stability, and perseverance.

Remember that *obstacles are really detours in the right direction*. Where others give up, you find you can carry on, manifest great things, and reap the rewards of your hard work. As you see this sweet spot, know you are balancing your Karmic Debt.

Karmic Debt Number 14/5 - Freedom

The Karmic Debt number 14/5 reveals an actual abuse of *freedom* in a previous lifetime. This means that you are now paying back for acting upon your selfish sense of personal freedom at the expense of other people. In a previous life, your irresponsibility, escapism, lack of accountability, overindulgence in sensual pleasures like food and sex, and addictive behaviors with drugs, alcohol, or gambling caused deep pain for another.

Since the infraction in the Karmic Debt is based on the numbers 4 and 5, in your current life, you are forced to adapt to the constantly changing circumstances and recklessness of the number 5 while juggling the opposite requirements of the number 4—discipline, responsibility, and goal-setting. You will be pulled to reconcile your free-spiritedness with the limitations of structure.

The person with the Karmic Debt number 14/5 will initially walk on the wild side and embody the more destructive elements of the number 5—the deep dive into addictions, broken promises and relationships, and the refusal to step up and handle any responsibility. These emotionally draining experiences will test you until you can master the lessons of the

5 and stay committed to your goals, no matter what is happening around you.

You are being asked to embrace the number 4 qualities of moderation in all its forms—discipline, routine, and order, while honoring the positive aspects of the number 5—fearlessness, fun, and flexibility. You will realize that pulling up the reins on yourself and setting some goals is the key to the *real* freedom you have been seeking.

Maybe you believe you have no idea how to focus and create a goal. You may feel organizing yourself is too tricky, restricting, and time-consuming. Maintaining order wherever you can in your life will take a concentrated effort. But you need to use your innate adaptability skills and create emotional stability so you are not tossed around by the unexpected changes going on all around you.

Taking responsibility for yourself and others, showing up on time, and not jumping from one thing to the next are required. You are called to embody the highest expression of the number 5—the social, sensual, adventurous spirit and **use your freedom in constructive, productive ways.**

Yours is a fearless, rollercoaster existence, but when you learn self-control and discipline, your freedom can soar. Allowing yourself periods of calm does not mean you are being fenced in. You can still live your life to the fullest with some guardrails in place. Keep your goals high, maintain your faith, and do not give up on yourself. That is how you work to balance your Karmic Debt.

Karmic Debt Number 16/7 - Love

The Karmic Debt number 16/7 points to an extreme misuse of *love* in a past lifetime. This means that you are now paying back for causing suffering to others through your actions in relationships. This includes illicit affairs, betrayals, irresponsibility, self-centeredness, indifference, cruelty and manipulation.

Since the infraction in the Karmic Debt is based on the numbers 6 and 7, in your current life, you will have a significant focus on family obligations, the pull to be in committed relationships, and the need to shoulder more responsibility as you get older. The 7 influence is the desire for introspection and isolation. You will experience this struggle as you try to make your intimate relationships work, yet you also feel pulled to be alone for soul-searching.

What this boils down to in the 16/7 is a leveling of an inflated ego. Selfish, inconsiderate actions in a previous life will cause you to deal with the fall of your ego in this life. You will find that you repeatedly face cycles of destruction of the old and birth of the new. Your big plans are challenged, situations collapse, and you feel resentment. You are continuously forced to accept change and the impermanence of life.

This could present as sudden betrayals, losing friendships, and dysfunctional relationships. However, when things are falling apart, this is a *cleansing of the ego*, allowing you to find new, healthy ways to relate to others. Your karmic goal is to balance the scales regarding relationships, so you are being shown how to work on your ability to express yourself emotionally and to show up authentically for others.

These intense relationship dramas can be a humbling experience. But it is all leading toward a *spiritual rebirth* for you. This is the influence of the number 7 in the 16/7 Karmic Debt. When things keep falling apart, the time has come for you to seek your spiritual center. This Karmic Debt number is the path of tremendous spiritual growth and moving toward a higher consciousness.

You will be given many opportunities to start fresh and revise your outlook on life. You must adapt to change and flow with the destruction and rebirth process. This will teach you to create new ways of dealing with relationship issues that feel positive for you and everyone else involved.

Though you will feel a constant pull to be involved with family and intimate relationships, this does not mean you must have a traditional family with a white picket fence to pay back your Karmic Debt. It is about understanding yourself, making peace with how you handle responsibility, giving love in your relationships—*and committing to doing it well.*

Work on your spiritual connection to a higher power, animals, and nature. When you come to trust that relationships are placed in your path for your own healing and spiritual growth, when you are taking responsibility and nurturing and mentoring others, then you are balancing your Karmic Debt.

Karmic Debt Number 19/1 - Power

The Karmic Debt number 19/1 indicates a severe abuse of *power* in a previous incarnation. This means you are now paying back for incredibly selfish and calculated behaviors you enacted from your position of strength. You lacked compassion for people in your care, knew what you were doing, and intentionally inflicted suffering on others.

Since the infraction is based on the numbers 9 and 1, you will learn the proper use of power in this current life. You will be challenged by people and situations where others attempt to control and overpower you. You will be tested until you genuinely embody the best characteristics of the number 1— empowered leadership, self-confident independence, originality and innovation, and resilience.

With the influence of the number 9, you will also be asked to infuse your leadership with integrity, compassion, and humanitarian concern. The 9 also represents losses, letting go, and selfless service to others. In this life, you are learning to assert yourself, claim your power, and discover that only using your creative abilities and energy for the greater good will satisfy you.

Some of the difficulties the Karmic Debt number 19/1 faces include overcoming challenges alone and often being left to stand alone. The number 1 is about not giving up when things go wrong and keeping your determination to succeed consistently high. In this lifetime, resilience will be necessary as your best efforts and good intentions seem to fall short of the mark repeatedly.

You will often feel the oppositional pull of the 1's negative traits. Instead of seeking healthy independence, you find yourself entangled in co-dependent relationships. You tend to lack confidence and ambition, failing to step into your natural leadership role and defaulting to a victim mentality. Look at these obstacles as detours on your way to empowered independence. Remember that you have a debt to pay; balancing it means walking a rockier road.

Learning to individuate and assert yourself can make you self-centered and egotistical, even unintentionally intimidating. You are meant to be a confident pioneer, but do not resort to bullying to get your way. This can include stubbornness and a refusal to accept help from others. The 1 learns self-sufficiency and makes decisions alone. Yet much of your aloneness is self-imposed; you don't want to take advice or listen to others' opinions.

Another lesson of the Karmic Debt 19/1 is to become available in your relationships, recognize the importance of interdependence, and accept help and support when needed. You are balancing your karmic debt by rewiring your beliefs about the self, independence, and achievement and by learning to use your power in selfless ways to help others on a grand scale.

Some people are afraid of what they might find if they try to analyze themselves too much, but you have to crawl into your wounds to discover where your fears are. Once the bleeding starts, the cleansing can begin.

— TORI AMOS

12

MATURITY NUMBER

You may not control all the events that happen to you, but you can decide not to be reduced by them.

— MAYA ANGELOU

Consider this your "mid-life crisis" number. This number kicks in sometime in your 30s–40s and gradually builds for the rest of your life. The Maturity number reflects your maturity and spiritual growth as you've moved past childhood issues and better understand your goals and where you're headed in life. You no longer waste time on things that don't reflect your identity.

There is no specific date for the onset of this number, but you will feel the energy pulling you in the early mid-life years. It feels like a message you keep hearing within, a siren call for something long buried that is now returning more fully into your awareness. The aspects of this number were evident in your youth, but over time, you lost sight of this goal.

Since the Maturity number combines your Life Path and Destiny/Expression numbers, it reveals how you merge your strengths with your challenges. You have reached an age where you are better aware of your talents and can steer yourself toward your dreams. The Maturity number is an exciting one to reach. You are finally letting your heart guide your path in life.

How to Calculate Your Maturity Number

As you slowly grow into your Life Path goals, through the channels of your Destiny/Expression number, you will find that this Maturity number becomes the ultimate destination. It is fitting, then, that the way to reach your Maturity number is by adding your Life Path and Destiny numbers together.

For example:
Life Path number 8
Destiny/Expression number 6
8 + 6 = 14
1 + 4 = 5
5 is the Maturity number.

Maturity Number 1

As you age, you will desire more independence and want to break away from dependent situations that curb your individuality. This may involve family or financial dependencies that make you feel limited. You think the time for recognition of your achievements is approaching, and you are ready to take charge. Maturity number 1 is less willing to accept failure and will fight for the honor you feel you deserve. You will be more determined to build an exciting, active, and adventurous life that reflects your innovative vision.

Maturity Number 2

As you mature, you'll find yourself called upon more and more to use tact and sensitivity to evaluate the motivations of others. You will find that your ability to understand people and wield influence through gentle guidance increases dramatically the older you get. Maturity number 2 has learned the art of discrimination and can intuit the motivations of others quite well. Working behind the scenes to build cooperative relationships may not get much public recognition. Still, you will feel great emotional satisfaction seeing the positive results and the harmony among people due to your influence.

Maturity Number 3

As you get older, your creativity and self-expression will fully bloom. You communicate more efficiently, and your artistic abilities will improve. You feel optimistic about your future and want to embrace life and your loved ones. If you are not already involved in creative pursuits, you will be inspired to write, act, paint, make music, or do anything that involves performing. Maturity number 3 may still deal with emotional extremes, but generally, you are more enthusiastic and joyful than ever. This is a very happy, blessed number to mature into.

Maturity Number 4

As you age, you will find yourself increasingly goal-oriented and being practical and organized to bring your ideas to fruition. Your later years will be a time of increased activity, and these efforts will bring you great rewards. Maturity number 4 will be less interested in retirement and slowing down because there is so much you still want to accomplish. Issues regarding limitations will be a recurring theme, requiring you to be flexible. Ultimately, your goal is to create something that will last that you can enjoy together with your family. Along the way, remember to congratulate yourself on a job well done and stop and smell the roses.

Maturity Number 5

As you get older, your energy begins to speed up. Freedom is what you want now. Adventure, new experiences, creativity—you want the time and resources to enjoy it all now. Your interests become more diverse, and you feel called to revel in all your physical senses. With Maturity number 5, there will be a shift in your life regarding your disciplined use of freedom. It would be best if you faced situations related to excessive, indulgent behaviors that limit your productivity. Ideally, in your later life, you will learn self-discipline, adapt to unexpected changes, and still enjoy much progress, excitement, and travel.

Maturity Number 6

As you mature, you will be increasingly called to provide care and comfort to others. The well-being of family and community becomes your focus. You will deal with increased responsibility, mentoring, advice-giving, and healing in your intimate relationships. You naturally step into the role of the family matriarch or patriarch. A solid financial foundation through sound planning or an inheritance is indicated with Maturity number 6. You can look forward to being very comfortable in your golden years at home with your loved ones.

Maturity Number 7

As you age, you need to understand yourself and contemplate the mysteries of life. You become very introspective and intuitive, focusing on widening your knowledge of spiritual matters. Maturity number 7 seeks the truth now, possibly brought on by a dramatic shift in life that makes you need more privacy and solitude to process your thoughts and feelings. You may need to make agreements with loved ones regarding your greater need for quiet contemplation. Ultimately, you can share your wisdom and insight into the secrets of life with others.

Maturity Number 8

You will be called upon to use your business acumen to achieve financial abundance in your later years. You find yourself more deeply committed to work and using your influence wisely. Maturity number 8 finds that difficulties in your path are much easier to navigate now. Issues around power and achievement come to the fore until you learn to cultivate balance and moderation with money. Some detachment from your material success is necessary; after all, you can't take it with you! You will learn the value of giving back and use your financial success to benefit humanity.

Maturity Number 9

As you mature, you become drawn to public service and championing a humanitarian cause. Maturity number 9 becomes increasingly concerned with having a role in making the world a better place, and international travel may be involved. You find a greater appreciation for art now and much beauty in nature. Understanding grows as you feel this spiritual calling to a higher purpose, and your self-centeredness fades. Forgiveness of self and others takes precedence. You can use your considerable talents to heal and teach, which brings you a profound sense of belonging.

Maturity Number 11/2

As you age, you will feel all the pull toward relationship sensitivity as the 2 Maturity number, with additional intuitive and psychic abilities. You are called to use your diplomacy in relationships and modulate the energies of the group. However, Maturity number 11/2 is moving toward a period of intense illumination and spiritual growth, and with that will come a shift in emotional sensitivity, including psychic gifts. You are focused on relationships and how you can feel spiritually empowered within them by practicing tolerance and acceptance.

Maturity Number 4/22

As you age, you reevaluate how to bring your grand visions to life best. The difficulties of your early life have eased, and your power and confidence have grown. Maturity number 4/22 has a higher sense of spiritual purpose, which brings more challenges, but now you have the experience and ability to keep pushing forward with your goals. Like the 4 Maturity number, you must work your way around limitations. Now, you realize you need to balance your desire to work with a need for self-care. You become more practical, yet you still have the ideal vision of building something on a grand scale that helps many people.

We are what we repeatedly do. Excellence, then, is not an act, but a habit.

— ARISTOTLE

13

RELATIONSHIP COMPATIBILITY NUMBERS

Love is not all you need. You need mutual respect. You need support. You need trust. You need boundaries. You need people to be there when it matters. You need space to grow and acceptance when you do. You need people to show their love in a way you can understand.

— NEDRA GLOVER TAWWAB

Numerology reveals a person's innate value system – what drives them, what matters most to them. Those who share similar values can more easily sustain a happy, healthy relationship through life's ups and downs. Once you know your numbers and those of your loved ones, you will see what matters most to each person.

Everyone is on their own personal journey to finding their highest selves. This can help you detach in some ways, take certain behaviors less personally, and accept your differences more readily. We cannot control everything in life, but we can control our reactions, and that self-awareness can significantly improve your relationships.

As the Law of Attraction states: *That which is like unto itself is drawn;* only that which matches your vibrational wavelength will come to you. And whatever you focus on will expand, whether you want it or not. Your focus determines your reality.

The thoughts you think determine the relationships you attract. You attract what you believe you deserve. You are a vibrational being, pulling to you what matches your point of attraction—the vibration you emit. When you are focused on someone's positive traits and behaviors, you are training yourself to continue to attract more positive aspects, more of what you desire to see in yourself and in those you are energetically pulling toward you.

When looking at potentials for success in relationships, the most significant factor is how much each person is in alignment with those positive, healthy qualities of their own Life Path number. Love and genuine connection are the most beautiful human experiences we can have. But until we are aware of our challenges, we may continue to expect others to provide the answers that can only be found within. Ultimately, we are responsible for our own fulfillment.

In reality, there are no "ideal compatibility" number pairings. As there are upsides and downsides to all the numbers, one way to gauge relationship compatibility is by seeing how well you and your partner handle the destructive tendencies of the Life Path mission. You will each keep encountering your obstacles, enacting the same relationship dynamics, until you become aware of them and can begin taking responsibility for your often unconscious behaviors.

People always come into our lives for a reason—we are here to help each other grow along the path of our life's purpose. We are all in our own stages of development. Unconsciously, we choose relationships that will challenge us. Relationships are our best teachers, deepening our self-awareness and helping us to release negative tendencies that restrict us from living our Life Path purpose. In that sense, all relationships can be seen as successful, no matter the duration of the connection.

That being said, seeing how you and your partner are each doing on your Life Paths can give you a sense of how you are flowing together and uncover areas of friction you can each work on to improve your relationship. All relationships require compromise; the goal is to constructively communicate your needs and feelings without losing your sense of self.

The most crucial factor for any healthy relationship is mutual respect. Without it, love just crumbles. Mutual respect means speaking to each other in a respectful and considerate way, communicating about joint decisions, communicating your needs clearly, and responding to your partner's needs with kindness and compassion.

This does not mean sacrificing yourself to meet their needs. Healthy boundaries bring ease and clarity to a relationship. Boundaries demonstrate your self-respect and respect for your partner. A boundary you set is not a rule for **another person** to obey. A boundary is your **own** rule for **yourself**, describing how **you** will respond if the other person behaves in hurtful ways. For example, here is one boundary you can set for yourself: "When you are yelling, I will not continue the conversation."

Conflict cannot survive without your participation.

— DR. WAYNE DYER

It takes practice to enforce your boundaries in emotional situations, and you must be able to communicate with love about complex issues with your partner. Relationships are not easy, but if something feels off or wrong to you, trust your intuition and explore what you are feeling. Know that your feelings are always valid and deserve attention and respect.

People show you who they are and how they feel about you by the way they treat you. Believe what they are showing you.

Remember that people behave in relationships based on the following:

We love based on our level of self-love.

We communicate based on our level of self-awareness.

We behave based on our level of healed trauma.

Take care of yourself first. Learn who you are and what makes your soul sing. Stare down your demons and make peace with them however you can. Never stop growing. Love yourself. Everything flows from that in a relationship.

Harmonizing all the energies in your numerology chart can be challenging, especially in predicting relationship success. The Life Path number may be the strongest indicator, but your Heart's Desire numbers (inner emotions) are the second most important indicator. You can also compare your Personality numbers (outer persona) and Destiny/Expression (your whole identity) numbers to see where you can focus your best energies in your relationship.

Familiarize yourself with your Life Path traits and your partner's. Remember that the Life Path takes a lifetime to achieve, so you will naturally swing between the positive and negative poles of your Life Path numbers over time. But it will help to remember your ultimate Life Path goals and consider how your awareness can assist your partner in accomplishing their goals.

Know that when you feel good and empowered, you are in vibrational alignment with your highest good. Numerology alone cannot predict the outcome of any relationship—nothing can do that. You have to trust your heart and your intuition. The universe and the numbers always guide you—and you can tell by how you feel. Stay in tune with yourself. And then your relationships can thrive.

Nobody on this earth has the right to tell anyone that their love for another human being is morally wrong.

— BARBRA STREISAND

Here are some key points to consider for each Life Path number in relationships:

Life Path 1 in Relationship

The 1 Life Path's mission is to learn about the self—who you are, follow your unique vision, and carve out your independent path. You naturally tend to be the leader in a relationship, so you need someone who supports your choices and praises your accomplishments. Sometimes, you lack confidence and need someone in your corner to lift you up.

This may lead you to choose partners who are more like students or followers in the relationship. You can be so focused on your goals that you may lack awareness of the other's needs and feelings. Work to release some of your "go it alone" mindset and let someone into your heart. Remember that your best partner will be your equal in every way. That way, you can learn true co-creation and how to give and take in a relationship.

Life Path 2 in Relationship

The 2 Life Path loves to be in love. The 2 feels whole when partnered up in an intimate relationship. You must feel emotionally safe enough to express yourself fully with your partner. Since you are so attuned to the emotions of others, you are super sensitive and can be easily hurt. You do not enjoy confrontation and often give in to avoid a fight.

Sometimes, you are so giving in a relationship that you lose your sense of self and tend to smother your partner. Bring the focus back to your own needs. Remember that you don't have to do it all or fulfill your partner's every whim. Good communication and strengthening your emotional boundaries will make for a healthier connection with your loved one.

Life Path 3 in Relationship

The 3 Life Path is fun-loving, passionate, and very expressive. The 3 can be dramatic and intense. You are a communicator and need to be heard in a relationship, so you need someone who is a caring, good listener. You are involved in many creative projects, and your attention can be quickly scattered.

The 3 lives in the moment, not planning much for tomorrow. Yet your intense emotions often keep you in a state of depression. You need encouragement to show your true feelings rather than skim the surface. You are at your best in a relationship when you are given the necessary support to work through your emotional traumas and find your equilibrium.

Life Path 4 in Relationship

The 4 Life Path wants stability and security in love. You love order and organization and want a partner who is as honest and reliable as you are. You want to feel comforted and supported, but you may not readily show your feelings to others. You tend to be the one who makes the rules and takes charge in the relationship.

The 4 has a stubborn streak and may have difficulty giving up control. Sometimes, you can be all work and no play, and you need to be gently encouraged to take some risks. You are at your best with your partner when you are flexible and willing to relax and have fun.

Life Path 5 in Relationship

The 5 Life Path is the ultimate adventurer, highly energetic, and the most sensual of the life paths. You crave experiences of all kinds. You need your space and freedom to experience everything the world offers.

Commitment in a relationship can be a challenge for you. You love the thrill of falling in love, yet you're a wild child who doesn't want to be fenced in by tradition. After your share of escapades, you will be ready for love, but only when you genuinely desire commitment.

Life Path 6 in Relationship

The 6 Life Path is designed for long-term commitment. You get deep satisfaction from being in a couple and feel lost at sea without your partner. Highly nurturing and responsible, you are a perfectionist with high expectations of your love.

Sometimes, your idealism about your partner can be unrealistic, and you tend to be difficult to please. Your need for control is strong, so to find that healthy partnership you crave, you need to be supportive of your partner and be sure to take good care of yourself as you do for others.

Life Path 7 in Relationship

The 7 Life Path is the analyst, the intellectual, and always seeking the truth. In a relationship, you may seem mysterious and have trust issues. It would be best to have time alone to process, think, and unplug.

Your task in a relationship is to get your head out of the clouds and not allow your intellect to override your emotions. For a healthy relationship, you need to communicate about your need for downtime and know that your partner accepts this, and you can return refreshed and ready to connect.

Life Path 8 in Relationship

The 8 Life Path seeks power and authority in all areas. Usually charming and successful, the 8 likes to shine and wants a partner on their arm who also presents well. You want someone to help you fulfill your personal empowerment goals and financial abundance.

Your task in a relationship is to give less attention to your business and more attention to your partner. Know that business may be booming, but money can't buy you love. Relax your need for control and allow yourself to open up emotionally to your partner.

Life Path 9 in Relationship

The 9 Life Path is charismatic, romantic, and giving to others. However, your ideals can be so high as to be unrealistic, and you like things done your way. The 9 can have trouble letting go of the past and items in general. You want to please your partner, but you find it hard to allow yourself to be vulnerable.

As giving as you are, you can sometimes be aloof and dwell on the past. The 9 doesn't like asking for help, so you need to work on letting your partner in, genuinely listening, and trusting the ebb and flow of life.

People will forget what you said, people will forget what you did, but people will never forget how you made them feel.

— MAYA ANGELOU

Numerology Personal Years

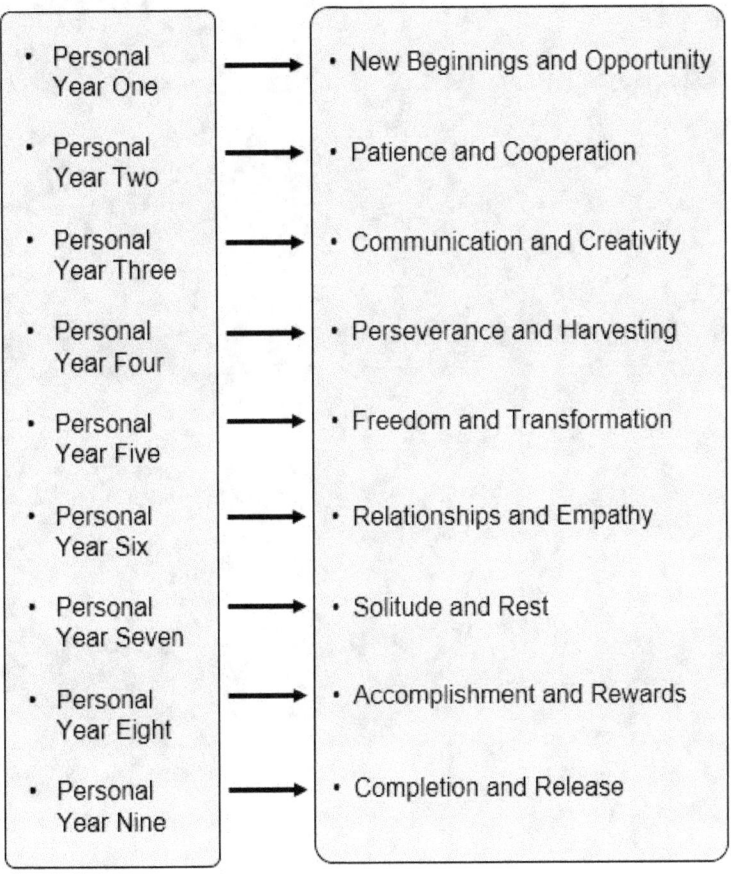

- Personal Year One → • New Beginnings and Opportunity
- Personal Year Two → • Patience and Cooperation
- Personal Year Three → • Communication and Creativity
- Personal Year Four → • Perseverance and Harvesting
- Personal Year Five → • Freedom and Transformation
- Personal Year Six → • Relationships and Empathy
- Personal Year Seven → • Solitude and Rest
- Personal Year Eight → • Accomplishment and Rewards
- Personal Year Nine → • Completion and Release

14

PERSONAL YEAR AND MONTH CYCLE NUMBERS

Every person, all the events of your life are there because you have drawn them there. What you choose to do with them is up to you.

— RICHARD BACH

In numerology, we repeatedly experience nine-year Personal Year cycles throughout our lifetime. Each year correlates to a number 1–9. When that cycle ends, we begin a new process of nine years. The Personal Years go from January 1 to December 31.

People always feel a profound energy shift at the end of each year, a collective transition pulling us into a brand new year—a clean slate. Each Personal Year has an important theme, with issues that will repeat throughout the year to offer innumerable chances for self-understanding and wisdom around that year's theme.

If we can face and overcome the challenges of the theme, then new opportunities enter the scene. When we fight or ignore our circumstances, similar situations will recur until we utilize these chances for real growth and expansion. Knowing your theme for each year is invaluable to accelerating the development of your consciousness.

Learning the theme of each Personal Year is essential so you can align yourself with the energy flowing rather than push against it. You have a better understanding of events and can access the deeper meaning. The energy of each year is powerful and can carry you forward to fantastic growth if you stay aware of what you are meant to focus on this year.

When your Personal Year number happens to match your Life Path number, expect the drama and intensity of the theme to increase. Remember that any challenges you experience are opportunities to strengthen any weak areas within that year's theme. Stay aligned with the goals of the year's theme, pay attention, and know that what may feel random has real meaning and purpose for you.

How to Calculate Your Personal Year Number

To determine your current Personal Year, you combine your birth month plus birth date plus the **current year** (not your birth year as you do for your Life Path number).

For example:

February 24, 2023

Month: 2

Day: 24

Year: 2024

Subtotal: 2050

Now, add the subtotal together. Keep adding until a single digit is obtained.

2 + 0 + 5 + 0 = 7

This adds up to being a **7 Personal Year.**

How to Calculate Your Personal Month Number

The energetic vibration of the year can also be calculated down to the energy for each month of that year. Then, you can see the theme of the overall year as well as the theme for any particular month of that year.

Keep in mind that September is a powerful month for every year because, for all Personal Years, September always matches the Personal Year number. For a Personal Year 2, September is always a 2 month. For Personal Year 8, September is always an 8 month, and so on. September of each year is when your Personal Year energies are at an all-time high, so use that focus to express and manifest your Personal Year theme to the fullest.

Find your Personal Year number as calculated above, adding your birth month, birth date, and **current year.**

Use your Personal Year number and add the month number to it.

January is the year's first month, so add the correct month number below to your Personal Year number.

January = 1
February = 2
March = 3
April = 4
May = 5
June = 6
July = 7
August = 8
September = 9
October = 10
November = 11
December = 12

For example:

January is the year's first month, so add 1 to your Personal Year number.

For a Personal Year 1, January will be a 2 month: Personal Year 1 + 1 (January is month 1) = 2.

You don't have to explain why you want what you want, do what you do, love what you love, need what you need. You are allowed to live a life some people don't understand.

— LAURA MCKOWEN

Personal Year 1

This starts a new nine-year cycle, a time of positive new beginnings, massive change, and the boundless energy necessary to bring your new visions to life. Your actions this year will significantly affect the course of the next nine years. If you ignore this chance to expand, there is a tendency to take the steam out of the whole phase of nine years. It will be hard to break if you establish an apathetic or listless habit this year.

These 12 months are devoted to creating a whole new phase and focus in your life. The 1 Year can have an enormous impact, so take advantage of this high energy and *run with it*. Align with this energy, and you will be carried forward. You will feel the power of this year and many new opportunities swirling around you month by month. Let this be your incentive.

This year emphasizes independence, individuality, courage, and self-reliance. It is time to clarify your goals and start working toward their achievement. Power is high this year, and it is a time to act.

There will be difficulties, but the year is designed to teach you lessons in trusting your initiative and creativity. You'll be given opportunities to assert your independence on every level. Vital changes are taking place within you, directing you to follow your feelings with courage and accept that complete change is necessary.

Last year (the 9 Year) brought an entire cycle of your life to a conclusion. It was an emotional year of endings, confusion, and learning to let go. You were starting to feel the pull to the new cycle, the confident energy of the 1 Year that is beginning now. Release any issues and limiting beliefs that still anchor you to the past. It's time to begin anew and plant the seeds that you want to see take root and grow over the next nine years.

The high power that the 1 Year carries cannot be underestimated. This is the start of significant changes that will unfold and propel you forward, which you will see culminate when the 9 year comes around. What do you want to achieve? What would be best for your long-term future? Change is coming. Even if you start small, take the steps necessary to move forward.

As you assert your independence, you may grapple with the opposite issues of dependence and times of loneliness. But do not get stuck in resentment and blame. Believe in yourself, accept the reality of your potential, and feel the natural self-confidence that arises from this.

You must begin something new and vital this year. Utilize the magic and momentum of the powerful 1 Year and take bold action!

Personal Year 2

After the high energy of the 1 Year, the 2 Year is a calmer, slower year where you can take a breather. Let your emotions flow freely, slow down, and relax. All situations will move more slowly this year, and pushing ahead with force will not bring the desired results. Patience and cooperation are the main themes in the 2 Year.

This year is focused on developing your relationships. You will strengthen your emotional boundaries and consider how you want to give and receive love. You are highly sensitive and intuitive now, and you are easily impatient with others. You will be given lessons about listening, understanding others, and tolerance.

Though things appear to be moving slowly, you must trust the timing in a 2 Year. You are tending to the seeds you planted last year. But be reassured that everything you need to succeed is gathering strength and unfolding behind the scenes. The 2 Year is an emotional sponge—you will naturally draw into yourself people, issues, and situations necessary for your growth. Your work is to quiet your mind and access your intuition to guide you to the right decisions.

As relationships are at the forefront now, networking and teamwork come into play. Here again, you will need to practice patience and focus on creating harmony to make progress forward. Practice living from moment to moment, staying in the present, so that you can feel for any changes that need to be made. Intimate relationships can take center stage. Focus on others and really become aware of how you are connected to them.

To accomplish your goals, you must keep your energy aligned with the cycle you are in. This is true for all Personal Years. As powerful as the 1 Year was, you cannot push yourself in the 2 Year, which does not utilize force or competition. Let things develop in their own time. Peace and cooperation are so necessary this year.

With this calmer pace, you will become frustrated with delays and circumstances that test your patience. Nonetheless, do not just surge ahead and try to break through more rapidly. Taking control of matters will only work against you during this phase.

In this slower, contemplative energy, you will learn much about yourself as you find harmony within your direction in life. Settle into yourself and flow with this nurturing energy that carries you along. Just flow with it. The progress you desire is gathering steam behind the scenes.

Personal Year 3

The 3 Year has a light, fun, and optimistic energy. You are finding your own voice, expressing yourself, and discovering what makes you happy. This year, you will be able to determine your true desires and know that, no matter how things appear, what you desire is really attainable.

This is a year of change and self-improvement. How can you improve yourself on many levels? You will face all your emotions—the good, the bad, and the ugly. It is time to accept these feelings, let them surface, and express them. Only when your darkest fears and pain are released will you create the space for the joy and happiness this year has in store. Let go of anything that weighs you down, and you will feel your spirit rise very quickly this year.

The 3 wants you to be creative—whether through art, writing, performance, or any other avenue that allows freedom of self-expression. Go ahead and speak your truth! There is buoyant energy running through this year that will carry you to new joys, laughter, and pleasure. Give yourself permission to enjoy yourself and be social.

As you put yourself out there to communicate, you step into the real, authentic you. Keep in mind that your words have heightened power this year. Express yourself in healthy ways. You will improve and transform yourself this year through positive communication and creativity. This is the year to do all the artistic, creative work flowing through you, and finding the best outlet to express yourself.

The flip side to the happy highs of the 3 Year is the deep emotional lows you will wrestle with now. Self-doubt, guilt, pessimism, and depression can come out of nowhere. Just know that you are learning self-acceptance, and the more love and kindness you can show yourself, the less you will look to others for approval. The 3 energy rapidly sends out your positive or negative vibrations, so you will notice that others are reflecting your feelings back to you much more this year.

As you deal with the mood swings of the 3 Year, you will look at the quality of communication in your relationships and how you each express your needs. You may even redefine your relationships in ways that allow healthy independence. This is the year to learn what you want and then create it.

Do whatever is necessary to put your own happiness first. Focus on what you desire and pursue your interests with passion. Your charisma is undeniable, and your power of attraction is magnetic. Take that lovely vibration and do more of whatever feels playful and joyful!

Personal Year 4

This is the year to get serious about your future and put in the hard work necessary to accomplish your long-term goals. It is critical in the 4 Year that you *define your direction* and work toward a specific goal. The 4 Year has so much practical, focused energy that you must know your destination in advance and then tenaciously follow the course. Otherwise, you run the risk of apathy, disorganization, and burnout.

The 4 wants you to slow down, get organized, and decide which projects you want to guide and nurture to fruition. You want to make your life easier and more satisfying, so it's time to lay down some solid foundations that you can depend upon in the long run. You must be efficient and orderly, and you must create new routines to further your purpose. Set up new systems you are responsible for that help you monitor your progress.

You are creating stability and security now, so be aware of health issues and prioritize self-care. You will need your strength this year, so plan time for exercise and allow yourself some downtime. The 4 Year is a slow and steady period, and concentrated effort is required, so pace yourself with all the work you will be juggling. You will be very productive and proud of all you accomplish when you go step by step and persevere.

The 4 Year also represents the healing of old family issues. You will be made aware of things that need to be resolved and handled differently in the realm of family, but this is worthwhile work that will bring you much peace and relief.

A keyword in the 4 Year is limitation. As you feel the challenges of career, health, and family, you will meet roadblocks. Often, you will feel that your path forward is strewn with obstacles you cannot overcome. The 4 Year asks you to consider every aspect of your life and look for new solutions to your restrictive circumstances. It is time to weed out the self-limiting beliefs and attitudes you know are not working for you. Take an honest look at what is holding you back and work to eliminate trivial distractions.

It is time to get your act together and implement those practical plans. With determination and effort, you will achieve breakthroughs and lay the foundation for the happier life you genuinely want to live.

Personal Year 5

Freedom, change, and adventure are coming at you at high speed this year in every possible way. Expect the unexpected. This 5 Year energy is loose, exciting, and unpredictable, so stay open to all the new experiences. Be flexible and adaptable to the whirlwind of possibilities that will engulf you.

There will be travel, escapism, and a real focus on sensuality and physical pleasures. New people and new experiences will surround you, and the energy will pull you to jump in, take a chance, and have fun with it. This is the time to experience life to the fullest.

The 5 Year explores all issues related to freedom, so naturally, you will be shown the areas in your life where you do not feel free so you can work to release those restrictions. Where is fear holding you back? Where do you feel stuck? You will be asked to step out of your comfort zone repeatedly this year. If you do not open the door to the many opportunities that are knocking, you will remain stagnant and go nowhere. The energy is pulling you. Wander off the beaten track and go exploring.

With the focus on freedom and indulgence, watch out for overindulgence—food, sex, drugs, alcohol, money—any excessive behavior that can feel like freedom but can also veer into addiction. Have fun, but take care of your body. Love and respect yourself as you enjoy all your physical senses.

The 5 Year is the **PIVOTAL YEAR.** You are halfway through your nine-year cycle. Four years are behind you, and four years are ahead. This is the turning point, the year of significant transitions and change. What happens this year will redirect your focus, setting you off in a direction you have never been before. And this new direction will define who you become over the next four years.

If you have worked hard in your 4 Year to set your goals into motion, you can now set out confidently and embrace this 5 Year of freedom, variety, and change.

Personal Year 6

The 6 Year is the time to evaluate all of your relationships and the role that responsibility plays within them. You will take a deep look at yourself and how you behave in relationships. How do you love? How do you want others to show love to you? Deep connections and all matters of the heart are highlighted this year.

This is an excellent year to attract a mate or to recommit and strengthen your existing relationship. If you've been considering marriage or engagement, this is the year that you may feel most ready to take the plunge. Conversely, your new awareness of relationships may lead you to realize that an ending or even a divorce is imminent. It is time to see relationships as they really are and evaluate your place within the dynamic.

Home and family are your priorities this year. You are drawn to the comfort of a warm and loving home, and to that end, you may be doing some remodeling, renovating, or even upgrading to a beautiful home that reflects the love you feel for your family.

Responsibility is the central theme around all relationships for the 6 Year. You will feel a sense of duty and obligation to others, and most certainly, you will be taking on a new responsibility with family or friends that will require compassion, sacrifice, and adjustment. You will mentor, serve and support others in whatever way is necessary. The 6 energy is magnetic, and people are drawn to you who sense that you can counsel or help them somehow.

With this sense of responsibility comes the need for **balance**. You must first take care of your own needs before assisting others. Health and healing are necessary. Take a close look at your motivations for taking on specific responsibilities. Guilt, fear, and a need for control may drive your actions. Be aware of your tendencies toward perfectionism and judgment. This year, you will learn that sometimes you have to say "no." Often, the best way to help others is to show them that they must be responsible for themselves.

The 6 Year will be about love—healing, acceptance, and finding the right balance of give and take so your relationships can thrive.

Personal Year 7

After focusing on everyone else's needs in the 6 Year, we come to the 7 Year and enter a year-long period of deep reflection, inner work, solitude, and tests of faith. You will seek privacy and a quiet space to think, research, and do general mental housecleaning.

Maybe you need this downtime to read, study, and really probe your inner depths. This is a time for spiritual growth, in what-ever way you perceive that. Your intuitive abilities are enhanced, buried emotions are surfacing, and you suddenly question everything you believe you need. This process will take all year, so allow yourself the time for this retreat. There is much planning, processing, and learning in store.

Turning inward may be hard on your relationships, so clear communication is critical this year so you don't withdraw from social life altogether. You may be difficult to understand during a 7 Year, so be sure to reach out to connect back to your loved ones. This is a heavier, slower cycle. It's a good time for therapy, energy work, and meditation. Plumbing the depths will bring up painful and confusing emotions, but it's time to dig deep and excavate to see where you want to focus next.

Beware of the opposite pull to avoid the deep internal work and instead superficially skim the surface of your awareness or zone out with distractions. Conversely, overanalyzing situa-tions can mean you already know the answer, but you are in denial and hope to uncover an easier solution. Be honest with yourself and admit if some aspects of your current life no longer feel natural or desirable.

You will use this period to figure out what kind of life feels right to you now and begin to plan what might be necessary to get it. This is the time to just *be*, not to *do*. Obviously, you must maintain your daily responsibilities, but this is not the time to push yourself to charge ahead with things. Slow down, and know that this allows you to plan a more realistic approach to your new goals despite the frustration. The power of reflection in the 7 Year illuminates the empty spaces in your life. Express and release the deep feelings that will arise, and you will be rewarded with sudden insights and unexpected and even beautiful answers.

Do what is necessary to plan for alone time in the 7 Year to process your thoughts and feelings. Face your fears, consider what approaches could use revision, and take stock of your talents and abilities. This inner work should reveal what makes your heart sing and where you want to place your focus from now on. The revelations you experience will teach you how perfect your life can become.

Personal Year 8

This 8 Year is all about your personal empowerment. Prosperity, material and financial gain, achievement—it's all on the menu and starts with you taking control and stepping into your power. You are ready to take charge after last year's reflection, inner work, and preparation.

The 8 Year jump starts the intense "three-year transition cycle," consisting of Personal Years 8–9–1. Personal Year 8 is about power and financial gain. Personal Year 9 brings endings and closure, and then Personal Year 1 launches you forward into the brand new cycle. The 8 is an amplifier, pumping up the energy of everything you experience this year: your focus, your strength, your achievements, and your rewards. Get clear on your intentions, then take the reins and take action.

It is said that you get what you want in the 8 Year. Do you know what you want? What defines success for you? It is time to decide what matters most—financial success, career, health, or relationships. The energy coursing through this year is so dynamic that you can feel yourself carried to success in your endeavors. This is the time to be tenacious and go after your dreams.

With the 8 theme of power, know that your sense of empowerment will be tested in order to strengthen your endurance. Whatever issues you have around abundance and strength will be thrust forward for you to deal with now. You will have to look at areas that are out of alignment and clear that negative energy. The dark side of the power of 8 is disempowerment, victimhood, enabling or domination, and bullying. Work on balancing these issues that block your way forward. The 8 Year wants you to step up and assert yourself, and you will be given many opportunities this year to take charge.

Real personal empowerment is balanced with love and compassion. You are called to take yourself seriously this year and apply consistent effort in business, but realize that true success is not material but a state of contentment and satisfaction, however you define it. The 8 Year will test you the most in your weakest places, but when you step up and push forward, the rewards will be grand indeed.

This is the year to use your confidence, influence, and courage. Know that you are in the right place at the right time to create the life you want to live. Believe that you can have what you want and ride the manifesting energy of the 8 Year.

Personal Year 9

The end of your 9-year cycle has arrived, which means you will focus on endings, completion, and letting go of things to create a space for positive changes. You will not be able to launch into next year's new beginnings until you have released everything you are clinging to that is holding you back. The 9 Year is here to help you heal, to excavate what needs to come up, feel the feelings you have been denying, and release them.

This dramatic, emotional year will touch on every aspect of your life. It is a time of surrender, transition, and transformation. The 9 Year will take you back to your past. You will review all the highs and lows of the 9-year cycle that is drawing to a close, as well as your distant past. What do you need to let go of emotionally, mentally, spiritually, and physically? What no longer serves a purpose and keeps you in denial or frozen at some long-ago phase of your development?

Releasing what you have outgrown will bring improvements and create a ripple effect of relief and joy you did not even realize was possible. As one door closes, another door opens, but only if you are willing to accept your reality and express those pent-up emotions that have kept you from real growth. Do not continue to make the same mistakes and use the same excuses. The 9 Year will force you to face whatever has been standing in the way of your forward movement.

It is said that whatever painful realities you refuse to release in the 9 Year will follow you into your next cycle, greatly hindering your spiritual expansion and momentum around the corner next year when the 1 Year comes barreling in. But nothing new can come to you until you accept whatever has happened to you and work to release it. Emotions are energy and must *move up and through you to be released*. When you block and repress them, the energy continues to seek an escape route to flow through, leading to depression and disease.

Be compassionate with yourself and with others this year. Let the 9 Year show you how much you have let guilt, fear, and blame push happiness away. Make room for new truths, forgiveness, and a newfound sense of peace. There will be losses to process, but do not avoid letting go of what you know must be released. Allow yourself to sit with the space that these changes create for a while. See the radiance of being in the present moment.

All the unfinished business and emotional housecleaning you do this year can leave you fearful of the unknown. This anxiety is natural. Use this time to get organized, sort out what no longer works for you, and make those important changes. Open yourself to new possibilities, spiritual expansion, and a newfound sense of *hope*.

The 9 Year will have you reflecting on endings and transitions, but you will also feel the natural growth and expansion that is born from this. Take stock of how far you've come on so many levels over the past nine years! Endings create new beginnings, and you will see some beautiful transformations occurring in many areas of your life. Many long-held dreams may come to fruition now.

You are built not to shrink down into less but to blossom into more.

— OPRAH WINFREY

15

PUTTING IT ALL TOGETHER

The universe is working through you. Keep in mind that your desires were lovingly given to you so you'd have an exciting purpose to carry out during your stint here on Earth. You're shining a light that makes it possible for others to see their true selves as well.

— JEN SINCERO, *YOU ARE A BADASS*

Now that you have the basics of numerology, notice how the meanings of the numbers apply in different contexts, and you will be able to see how the numbers really are guiding you. Now you know what your soul intended to work on during this incarnation, and you can be fully on board with the plan as it unfolds for you.

Here is an example of using your numerology chart to gain insight into your spiritual progress and make more informed choices that serve your higher purpose.

This is an interpretation of my own core numbers. (For those who know me well, this analysis will surprise no one.)

8 -   Life Path number

6 -   Destiny/Expression number

11/2 -   Heart's Desire number

4 -   Personality number

5 -   Birthday Gift number

5 -   Maturity number

14/5-   Karmic Debt number

3 -   Personal Year number

Remember that your Destiny/Expression number explains HOW you will accomplish the WHAT of your Life Path goals. Your Birthday Gift number is an extra boost in helping you on your Life Path.

In this example, your Destiny/Expression number 6 will guide your lifelong walk to achieve your 8 Life Path. The 6 focuses on family responsibilities, serving others, and creating a warm home environment. The 8 is all about power, authority, and abundance. In this life, you will learn about the 8 personal power and sound financial management from your 6, through responsibilities toward family and loved ones.

Recall that there are two poles to the traits of each number—the positive and the negative. Achieving the goals of the Life Path number takes a lifetime to accomplish. We choose our Life Path precisely because our soul wants to grow and improve in this area. Generally, we start our path at the opposing end of the pole and slowly work our way up to owning the positive aspects of our Life Path number.

In this chart, you will often experience the OPPOSITE pole of your 8 Life Path. Instead of power and abundance, you will feel disempowered, wallowing in victimhood from a sense of scarcity. Throughout your life, you will be given endless opportunities to make better choices around this subject. Your Destiny/Expression number 6 issues will show you HOW you can grow into your 8 power traits.

Maybe you are overly involved and responsible for your family members (6 Destiny/Expression number), especially financially. Creating better boundaries and modulating your sense of responsibility is how you EMPOWER yourself, create FINANCIAL ABUNDANCE for yourself, and manage your AUTHORITY better (all your 8 Life Path goals, done through your 6 Destiny/Expression number).

As you consciously lean toward the **positive** aspects of your 6 Destiny/Expression number (modulating responsibility, being less judgmental and controlling), you ALSO naturally move into the **positive** aspects of your 8 Life Path number (management with ethical integrity, using your influence and power to assist others). You are constantly being presented with choices for your Destiny/Expression number (6, family responsibility), and you get to use your free will to decide if you want to react negatively or positively. How you choose reflects your progress forward on your Life Path.

Your Birthday number 5 will nudge you toward freedom, taking creative risks, and enjoying life to the fullest. These traits apply well to your Life Path 8 of learning to empower yourself, achieve material success, and live abundantly.

You will also use your Heart's Desire number (your deep inner feelings) to guide your choices. Your Heart's Desire number 11/2 is intuitive/spiritual sensitivity, focusing on intimate relationships. This dovetails nicely with your 6 Destiny/Expression number of focus on family responsibilities.

Your Personality number of 4 (how others perceive you) displays your knack for organization, a focus on details, and hard work to build a solid foundation.

Putting your core numbers together, you see that your main focus in life is emotional sensitivity, relationships, cooperation, and family responsibilities, and the desire to build your cozy home environment. Your 8 Life Path draws you toward financial abundance, empowering yourself around money, and stepping into your natural leadership abilities—all of which will come through emotional family issues for you. This will not materialize for you until later in life.

Your Maturity number is the sum of your Destiny/Expression and Life Path numbers (6 + 8 = 5). In your mid-life period, around your 40s, your Maturity number 5 will kick in and grow for the remainder of your life. Note that the 5 also happens to be your Birthday Gift number.

In this example, you will find that as you work to empower yourself through your responsible family issues, you will feel the energies of your Birthday number 5 AND your Maturity number 5 calling you toward … *freedom* from responsibility, adventure, travel, and indulging the senses. So, as you get older, after a lifetime of caring for others and financial struggle, the energies of risk-taking and fearlessness will come into play.

Here, too, be aware of both poles of the Maturity number. In this case, the 5 is all about change and new exciting life experiences, but the flip side is a tendency toward excess, overindulgence, and irresponsibility. The Maturity number is long-term energy playing out slowly in your later life over several decades, so keep an eye out for how you can utilize the new energy most productively when the time comes.

Your Karmic Debt of 14/5 continues the theme of impatience, impulsivity and the need for emotional stability through unexpected change. You need to learn moderation and flexibility to balance abuses of freedom in a past life.

In your present, you are always dealing with the energies of your Personal Year that you can use to your great advantage. In this chart, you are in a 3 Personal Year that asks you to be lighter, more social, and tap into your creativity and joyful self-expression.

This is my chart… so have I mastered all of that? Not yet! But I am aware of my lessons and I have made significant strides in these areas. So will you. Be good to yourself along your road to renewal.

There are three ways to ultimate success:

The first way is to be kind.

The second way is to be kind.

The third way is to be kind.

— MISTER ROGERS

16

FINAL THOUGHTS

Everything will be okay in the end. If it isn't okay, it isn't the end.

— PAULO COELHO

What I hope for you is that this book helps you build emotional awareness, inner strength, and the courage to walk your path with confidence. I hope what you have learned in your chart profoundly resonates with you and helps you direct your focus and goals. I hope it inspires you to dive deeper into any or all of the subjects discussed here—psychology, numerology, the afterlife, reincarnation, and the Law of Attraction.

Numerology is your life map, and you have your free will. You now understand your identity, instincts, general purpose, and what you came here to learn. There are any number of roads you can take to fulfill your purpose. There are no wrong turns here. It takes as long as it takes to embody your Life Path. Growth is guaranteed.

Remember who you really are—a divine being of eternal light. You are not the voice in your head, chattering away endlessly. You are separate from the voice. You are the one who observes the voice and can quiet your mind into stillness.

As you progress along your Life Path, practice returning to the present moment. Breathe, drop your resistance to whatever is happening, and flow with it. Meditation is the best tool to connect with your soul and spirit guides.

There's no wrong way to meditate. Just focus on something that feels good, breathe deeply, and imagine gently swiping away the repetitive intrusive thoughts. Return your focus to your breathing, allowing yourself to become still. It is only in the stillness that you can truly receive intuitive messages.

Even if you spend just 5 minutes continually swiping away thoughts that intrude, that is a successful meditation session. You are training your mind to seek the stillness your body and soul need to recharge.

Make more decisions – be intentional about where you flow your powerful, precious energy.

So why did your beautiful soul come to this crazy planet?

Growth. Spiritual expansion. Learning. Experiencing life in **all** its forms, emotions, and intensity. Reveling in your five senses, as you can only do embodied as a human, which your soul wanted to do very much.

Love. Love. Love. You are here to love yourself and love others. To feel love, teach love, and be love because you embody the Source of Love, the Creator of the Universe. You are so very loved. You wanted to shine your light of love into every dark corner of this planet. For every person you touch with love, the universe radiates that love exponentially, so everyone is lifted by it.

Love makes your soul crawl out from its hiding place.

— ZORA NEALE HURSTON

The afterlife, your natural home, is unconditional love, beautiful bliss beyond description, but incarnation…? *This is the Big Show, folks!* It's glorious, joyous, gritty, heartbreaking, extreme, and yes—you can't wait to get the heck out for much of your stay here. Then, after a rest period between lives, you can't wait to jump right back in. You want your ticket to the rollercoaster ride again. And again.

Your soul wasn't scared of life on Earth. This life is a stage play, an illusion, and over before you know it. So taste the ice cream, bury your face in your cat's warm fur, and listen to beautiful music that makes you weep. Breathe in the stunning art, the books, the sky at dusk. See as much of the beauty on this planet as you can.

Keep your heart open, tirelessly lift yourself out of despair, and keep going. Never give up. The person you will become in a few years is counting on you.

Remember that you are not alone—you are here co-creating with the universe, with Source Energy! You have a concierge in the sky responding to your vibration! You will always be given what you need to do the job you came to do.

You are the creator of your own reality, on a fantastic journey, and your life on Earth is essential.

Love and savor every juicy bit of your human life. Have fun with this.

Eat ALL the chocolate...

Grab the reins of your life and dance with the universe.

You are here to enable the divine purpose of the universe to unfold. That is how important you are.

— ECKHART TOLLE

YOUR ROLE IN SOMEONE ELSE'S JOURNEY

You called this book into your awareness by the Law of Attraction, and the universe delivered just what you needed.

Simply by sharing your honest opinion of this book and a little about your own experience, you'll make it easy for new readers to find the information they're looking for.

Thank you! Your review will have more impact than you might imagine.

Scan the QR code below to leave your review on Amazon.

REFERENCES

Eben Alexander, M.D., *Proof of Heaven: A Neurosurgeon's Journey into the Afterlife* (Simon & Schuster, 2012).

Felicia Bender, Ph.D., *The Ultimate Guide to Practical Numerology: Mapping Your Path & Purpose* (FAB Enterprises, Ltd., 2022).

Sandra Champlain, *We Don't Die A Skeptic's Discovery of Life After Death* (Morgan James Publishing, 2013).

Hans Decoz, *Numerology: The Key to Your Inner Self* (Penguin Random House, 1994).

Christine Delorey, *Life Cycles: Your Emotional Journey to Freedom and Happiness* (Osmos Books, 2000).

Elizabeth Gilbert, *Eat, Pray, Love* (Riverhead Books, 2007).

Esther and Jerry Hicks, *The Law of Attraction: The Basics of the Teachings of Abraham* (Hay House, Inc., 2006).

Michael Newton, Ph.D., *Journey of Souls: Case Studies of Life Between Lives* (Llewellyn Publications, 1995).

Violet Roy, *The Little Book of Numerology: The Science of Names, Numbers & The Law of Vibration* (Independently Published, 2022).

Robert Schwartz, *Your Soul's Plan: Discovering the Real Meaning of the Life You Planned Before You Were Born* (Frog Books/North Atlantic Books, 2009).

Cheryl Strayed, *Brave Enough* (Alfred A. Knopf, 2015).

Brian L. Weiss, M.D., *Many Lives, Many Masters: The True Story of a Prominent Psychiatrist, His Young Patient, and The Past-Life Therapy That Changed Both Their Lives* (Simon & Schuster, 1988).

Delphina Woods, *The Ultimate Numerology Book: The Complete Guide to the Spiritual Meaning of Numbers Including How Your Birthday and Name Affect Your Life Path* (Hentopan Publishing, 2022).